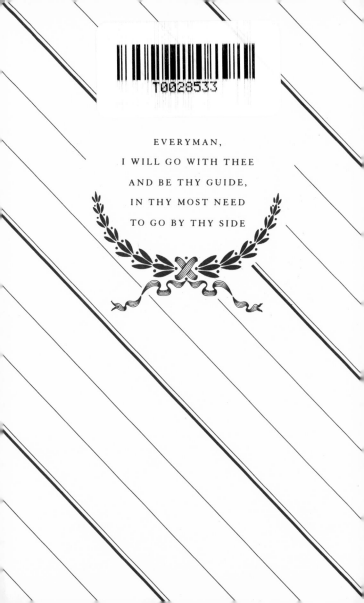

EVERYMAN,
I WILL GO WITH THEE
AND BE THY GUIDE,
IN THY MOST NEED
TO GO BY THY SIDE

EVERYMAN'S LIBRARY
POCKET POETS

Plath

Poems

Selected by
Diane Wood Middlebrook

EVERYMAN'S LIBRARY

POCKET POETS

Alfred A. Knopf · New York · Toronto

THIS IS A BORZOI BOOK

PUBLISHED BY ALFRED A. KNOPF

This selection by Diane Wood Middlebrook first published in
Everyman's Library, 1998

Twenty-second printing

Published by arrangement with HarperCollins Publishers, Inc.

'Barren Woman' and 'Song for a Summer's Day' originally appeared in
The New York Times Book Review.

www.randomhouse.com/everymans

ISBN 978-0-375-40464-1

Typography by Peter B. Willberg

Typeset in the UK by AccComputing, North Barrow, Somerset

Printed and bound in Germany by GGP Media GmbH, Pössneck

SYLVIA PLATH

CONTENTS

JUVENILIA

JILTED

My thoughts are crabbed and sallow,
    My tears like vinegar,
Or the bitter blinking yellow
    Of an acetic star.

Tonight the caustic wind, love,
    Gossips late and soon,
And I wear the wry-faced pucker of
    The sour lemon moon.

While like an early summer plum,
    Puny, green, and tart,
Droops upon its wizened stem
    My lean, unripened heart.

BLUEBEARD

I am sending back the key
that let me into bluebeard's study;
because he would make love to me
I am sending back the key;
in his eye's darkroom I can see
my X-rayed heart, dissected body:
I am sending back the key
that let me into bluebeard's study.

TRIO OF LOVE SONGS

(1)

Major faults in granite
  mark a mortal lack,
yet individual planet
  directs all zodiac.

Diagram of mountains
  graphs a fever chart,
yet astronomic fountains
  exit from the heart.

Tempo of strict ocean
  metronomes the blood,
yet ordered lunar motion
  proceeds from private flood.

Drama of each season
  plots doom from above,
yet all angelic reason
  moves to our minor love.

(2)

My love for you is more
     athletic than a verb,
agile as a star
     the tents of sun absorb.

Treading circus tightropes
     of each syllable,
the brazen jackanapes
     would fracture if he fell.

Acrobat of space,
     the daring adjective
plunges for a phrase
     describing arcs of love.

Nimble as a noun
     he catapults in air;
a planetary swoon
     could climax his career,

but adroit conjunction
     eloquently shall
link to his lyric action
     a periodic goal.

(3)

If you dissect a bird
   to diagram the tongue,
you'll cut the chord
   articulating song.

If you flay a beast
   to marvel at the mane,
you'll wreck the rest
   from which the fur began.

If you assault a fish
   to analyse the fin,
your hands will crush
   the generating bone.

If you pluck out my heart
   to find what makes it move,
you'll halt the clock
   that syncopates our love.

LAMENT

A VILLANELLE

The sting of bees took away my father
  who walked in a swarming shroud of wings
and scorned the tick of the falling weather.

Lightning licked in a yellow lather
  but missed the mark with snaking fangs:
the sting of bees took away my father.

Trouncing the sea like a raging bather,
  he rode the flood in a pride of prongs
and scorned the tick of the falling weather.

A scowl of sun struck down my mother,
  tolling her grave with golden gongs,
but the sting of bees took away my father.

He counted the guns of god a bother,
  laughed at the ambush of angels' tongues,
and scorned the tick of the falling weather.

O ransack the four winds and find another
  man who can mangle the grin of kings:
the sting of bees took away my father
who scorned the tick of the falling weather.

TWO LOVERS AND A BEACHCOMBER
BY THE REAL SEA

Cold and final, the imagination
    Shuts down its fabled summer house;
Blue views are boarded up; our sweet vacation
    Dwindles in the hour-glass.

Thoughts that found a maze of mermaid hair
    Tangling in the tide's green fall
Now fold their wings like bats and disappear
    Into the attic of the skull.

We are not what we might be; what we are
    Outlaws all extrapolation
Beyond the interval of now and here:
    White whales are gone with the white ocean.

A lone beachcomber squats among the wrack
    Of kaleidoscopic shells
Probing fractured Venus with a stick
    Under a tent of taunting gulls.

No sea-change decks the sunken shank of bone
    That chuckles in backtrack of the wave;
Though the mind like an oyster labors on and on,
    A grain of sand is all we have.

Water will run by rule; the actual sun
    Will scrupulously rise and set;
No little man lives in the exacting moon
    And that is that, is that, is that.

EPITAPH IN THREE PARTS

(1)

Rocking across the lapis lazuli sea
   comes a flock of bottle battleships
each with a telegram addressed to me.

'Destroy your mirror and avoid mishaps,'
   chirps the first; 'live on a silent island
where the water blots out all footsteps.'

The second sings: 'Receive no roving gallant
   who seeks to dally in the port till dawn,
for your fate involves a dark assailant.'

The third cries out as all the ships go down:
'There is more than one good way to drown.'

(2)

In the air above my island flies
   a crowd of shining gulls that plunge to launch
an accurate assault upon the eyes

of the bold sailor falling under drench
   and hunger of the surf that plucks the land,
devouring green gardens inch by inch.

Blood runs in a glissando from the hand
　　that lifts to consecrate the sunken man.
Aloft, a lone gull halts upon the wind,

announcing after glutted birds have flown:
'There is more than one good way to drown.'

(3)

Grasshopper goblins with green pointed ears
　　caper on leafstalk legs across my doorsill,
and mock the jangling rain of splintered stars.

My room is a twittering gray box with a wall
　　there and there and there again, and then
a window which proves the sky sheer rigmarole

that happens to conceal the lid of one
　　enormous box of gray where god has gone
and hidden all the bright angelic men.

A wave of grass engraves upon the stone:
'There is more than one good way to drown.'

1956

CHANNEL CROSSING

On storm-struck deck, wind sirens caterwaul;
With each tilt, shock and shudder, our blunt ship
Cleaves forward into fury; dark as anger,
Waves wallop, assaulting the stubborn hull.
Flayed by spray, we take the challenge up,
Grip the rail, squint ahead, and wonder how
     much longer

Such force can last; but beyond, the neutral view
Shows, rank on rank, the hungry seas advancing.
Below, rocked havoc-sick, voyagers lie
Retching in bright orange basins; a refugee
Sprawls, hunched in black, among baggage, wincing
Under the strict mask of his agony.

Far from the sweet stench of that perilous air
In which our comrades are betrayed, we freeze
And marvel at the smashing nonchalance
Of nature: what better way to test taut fiber
Than against this onslaught, these casual blasts of ice
That wrestle with us like angels; the mere chance

Of making harbor through this racketing flux
Taunts us to valor. Blue sailors sang that our journey
Would be full of sun, white gulls, and water drenched

With radiance, peacock-colored; instead, bleak rocks
Jutted early to mark our going, while sky
Curded over with clouds and chalk cliffs blanched

In sullen light of the inauspicious day.
Now, free, by hazard's quirk, from the common ill
Knocking our brothers down, we strike a stance
Most mock-heroic, to cloak our waking awe
At this rare rumpus which no man can control:
Meek and proud both fall; stark violence

Lays all walls waste; private estates are torn,
Ransacked in the public eye. We forsake
Our lone luck now, compelled by bond, by blood,
To keep some unsaid pact; perhaps concern
Is helpless here, quite extra, yet we must make
The gesture, bend and hold the prone man's head.

And so we sail toward cities, streets and homes
Of other men, where statues celebrate
Brave acts played out in peace, in war; all dangers
End: green shores appear; we assume our names,
Our luggage, as docks halt our brief epic; no debt
Survives arrival; we walk the plank with strangers.

ODE FOR TED

From under crunch of my man's boot
green oat-sprouts jut;
he names a lapwing, starts rabbits in a rout
legging it most nimble
to sprigged hedge of bramble,
stalks red fox, shrewd stoat.

Loam-humps, he says, moles shunt
up from delved worm-haunt;
blue fur, moles have; hefting chalk-hulled flint
he with rock splits open
knobbed quartz; flayed colors ripen
rich, brown, sudden in sunglint.

For his least look, scant acres yield:
each finger-furrowed field
heaves forth stalk, leaf, fruit-nubbed emerald;
bright grain sprung so rarely
he hauls to his will early;
at his hand's staunch hest, birds build.

Ringdoves roost well within his wood,
shirr songs to suit which mood
he saunters in; how but most glad
could be this adam's woman
when all earth his words do summon
leaps to laud such man's blood!

SONG FOR A SUMMER'S DAY

Through fen and farmland walking
With my own country love
I saw slow flocked cows move
White hulks on their day's cruising;
Sweet grass sprang for their grazing.

The air was bright for looking:
Most far in blue, aloft,
Clouds steered a burnished drift;
Larks' nip and tuck arising
Came in for my love's praising.

Sheen of the noon sun striking
Took my heart as if
It were a green-tipped leaf
Kindled by my love's pleasing
Into an ardent blazing.

And so, together, talking,
Through Sunday's honey-air
We walked (and still walk there –
Out of the sun's bruising)
Till the night mists came rising.

TWO SISTERS OF PERSEPHONE

Two girls there are: within the house
One sits; the other, without.
Daylong a duet of shade and light
Plays between these.

In her dark wainscoted room
The first works problems on
A mathematical machine.
Dry ticks mark time

As she calculates each sum.
At this barren enterprise
Rat-shrewd go her squint eyes,
Root-pale her meager frame.

Bronzed as earth, the second lies,
Hearing ticks blown gold
Like pollen on bright air. Lulled
Near a bed of poppies,

She sees how their red silk flare
Of petaled blood
Burns open to sun's blade.
On that green altar

Freely become sun's bride, the latter
Grows quick with seed.
Grass-couched in her labor's pride,
She bears a king. Turned bitter

And sallow as any lemon,
The other, wry virgin to the last,
Goes graveward with flesh laid waste,
Worm-husbanded, yet no woman.

FAUN

Haunched like a faun, he hooed
From grove of moon-glint and fen-frost
Until all owls in the twigged forest
Flapped black to look and brood
On the call this man made.

No sound but a drunken coot
Lurching home along river bank.
Stars hung water-sunk, so a rank
Of double star-eyes lit
Boughs where those owls sat.

An arena of yellow eyes
Watched the changing shape he cut,
Saw hoof harden from foot, saw sprout
Goat-horns. Marked how god rose
And galloped woodward in that guise.

LETTER TO A PURIST

That grandiose colossus who
Stood astride
The envious assaults of sea
(Essaying, wave by wave,
Tide by tide,
To undo him, perpetually),
Has nothing on you,
O my love,

O my great idiot, who
With one foot
Caught (as it were) in the muck-trap
Of skin and bone,
Dithers with the other way out
In preposterous provinces of the madcap
Cloud-cuckoo,
Agawp at the impeccable moon.

ALICANTE LULLABY

In Alicante they bowl the barrels
Bumblingly over the nubs of the cobbles
Past the yellow-paella eateries,
Below the ramshackle back-alley balconies,
    While the cocks and hens
    In the roofgardens
Scuttle repose with crowns and cackles.

Kumquat-colored trolleys ding as they trundle
Passengers under an indigo fizzle
Needling spumily down from the wires:
Alongside the sibilant harbor the lovers
    Hear loudspeakers boom
    From each neon-lit palm
Rumbas and sambas no ear-flaps can muffle.

O Cacophony, goddess of jazz and of quarrels,
Crack-throated mistress of bagpipes and cymbals,
Let be your *con brios*, your *cápricciosos*,
Crescendos, cadenzas, prestos and *prestissimos*,
    My head on the pillow
    (*Piano, pianissimo*)
Lullayed by susurrous lyres and viols.

WREATH FOR A BRIDAL

What though green leaves only witness
Such pact as is made once only; what matter
That owl voice sole 'yes', while cows utter
Low moos of approve; let sun surpliced in brightness
Stand stock still to laud these mated ones
Whose stark act all coming double luck joins.

Couched daylong in cloisters of stinging nettle
They lie, cut-grass assaulting each separate sense
With savor; coupled so, pure paragons of constance,
This pair seek single state from that dual battle.
Now speak some sacrament to parry scruple
For wedlock wrought within love's proper chapel.

Call here with flying colors all watchful birds
To people the twigged aisles; lead babel tongues
Of animals to choir: 'Look what thresh of wings
Wields guard of honor over these!' Starred with words
Let night bless that luck-rooted mead of clover
Where, bedded like angels, two burn one in fever.

From this holy day on, all pollen blown
Shall strew broadcast so rare a seed on wind
That every breath, thus teeming, set the land
Sprouting fruit, flowers, children most fair in legion
To slay spawn of dragon's teeth: speaking this promise,
Let flesh be knit, and each step hence go famous.

FIESTA MELONS

In Benidorm there are melons,
Whole donkey-carts full

Of innumerable melons,
Ovals and balls,

Bright green and thumpable
Laced over with stripes

Of turtle-dark green.
Choose an egg-shape, a world-shape,

Bowl one homeward to taste
In the whitehot noon:

Cream-smooth honeydews,
Pink-pulped whoppers,

Bump-rinded cantaloupes
With orange cores.

Each wedge wears a studding
Of blanched seeds or black seeds

To strew like confetti
Under the feet of

This market of melon-eating
Fiesta-goers.

SPIDER

Anansi, black busybody of the folktales,
You scuttle out on impulse
Blunt in self-interest
As a sledge hammer, as a man's bunched fist,
Yet of devils the cleverest
To get your carousals told:
You spun the cosmic web: you squint from center field.

Last summer I came upon your Spanish cousin,
Notable robber baron,
Behind a goatherd's hut:
Near his small stonehenge above the ants' route,
One-third ant-size, a leggy spot,
He tripped an ant with a rope
Scarcely visible. About and about the slope

Of his redoubt he ran his nimble filament,
Each time round winding that ant
Tighter to the cocoon
Already veiling the gray spool of stone
From which coils, caught ants waved legs in
Torpid warning, or lay still
And suffered their livelier fellows to struggle.

Then briskly scaled his altar tiered with tethered ants,
Nodding in a somnolence
Appalling to witness,
To the barbarous outlook, from there chose
His next martyr to the gross cause
Of concupiscence. Once more
With black alacrity bound round his prisoner.

The ants – a file of comers, a file of goers –
Persevered on a set course
No scruple could disrupt,
Obeying orders of instinct till swept
Off-stage and infamously wrapped
Up by a spry black deus
Ex machina. Nor did they seem deterred by this.

SPINSTER

Now this particular girl
During a ceremonious April walk
With her latest suitor
Found herself, of a sudden, intolerably struck
By the birds' irregular babel
And the leaves' litter.

By this tumult afflicted, she
Observed her lover's gestures unbalance the air,
His gait stray uneven
Through a rank wilderness of fern and flower.
She judged petals in disarray,
The whole season, sloven.

How she longed for winter then! –
Scrupulously austere in its order
Of white and black
Ice and rock, each sentiment within border,
And heart's frosty discipline
Exact as a snowflake.

But here – a burgeoning
Unruly enough to pitch her five queenly wits
Into vulgar motley –
A treason not to be borne. Let idiots

Reel giddy in bedlam spring:
She withdrew neatly.

And round her house she set
Such a barricade of barb and check
Against mutinous weather
As no mere insurgent man could hope to break
With curse, fist, threat
Or love, either.

BLACK ROOK IN RAINY WEATHER

On the stiff twig up there
Hunches a wet black rook
Arranging and rearranging its feathers in the rain.
I do not expect a miracle
Or an accident

To set the sight on fire
In my eye, nor seek
Any more in the desultory weather some design,
But let spotted leaves fall as they fall,
Without ceremony, or portent.

Although, I admit, I desire,
Occasionally, some backtalk
From the mute sky, I can't honestly complain:
A certain minor light may still
Lean incandescent

Out of kitchen table or chair
As if a celestial burning took
Possession of the most obtuse objects now and then
Thus hallowing an interval
Otherwise inconsequent

By bestowing largesse, honor,
One might say love. At any rate, I now walk
Wary (for it could happen
Even in this dull, ruinous landscape); skeptical,
Yet politic; ignorant

Of whatever angel may choose to flare
Suddenly at my elbow. I only know that a rook
Ordering its black feathers can so shine
As to seize my senses, haul
My eyelids up, and grant

A brief respite from fear
Of total neutrality. With luck,
Trekking stubborn through this season
Of fatigue, I shall
Patch together a content

Of sorts. Miracles occur,
If you care to call those spasmodic
Tricks of radiance miracles. The wait's begun again,
The long wait for the angel,
For that rare, random descent.

1957

HARDCASTLE CRAGS

Flintlike, her feet struck
Such a racket of echoes from the steely street,
Tacking in moon-blued crooks from the black
Stone-built town, that she heard the quick air ignite
Its tinder and shake

A firework of echoes from wall
To wall of the dark, dwarfed cottages.
But the echoes died at her back as the walls
Gave way to fields and the incessant seethe of grasses
Riding in the full

Of the moon, manes to the wind,
Tireless, tied, as a moon-bound sea
Moves on its root. Though a mist-wraith wound
Up from the fissured valley and hung shoulder-high
Ahead, it fattened

To no family-featured ghost,
Nor did any word body with a name
The blank mood she walked in. Once past
The dream-peopled village, her eyes entertained
    no dream,
And the sandman's dust

Lost luster under her footsoles.
The long wind, paring her person down
To a pinch of flame, blew its burdened whistle
In the whorl of her ear, and like a scooped-out
    pumpkin crown
Her head cupped the babel.

All the night gave her, in return
For the paltry gift of her bulk and the beat
Of her heart, was the humped indifferent iron
Of its hills, and its pastures bordered by black stone set
On black stone. Barns

Guarded broods and litters
Behind shut doors; the dairy herds
Knelt in the meadow mute as boulders;
Sheep drowsed stoneward in their tussocks of wool,
    and birds,
Twig-sleeping, wore

Granite ruffs, their shadows
The guise of leaves. The whole landscape
Loomed absolute as the antique world was
Once, in its earliest sway of lymph and sap,
Unaltered by eyes,

Enough to snuff the quick
Of her small heat out, but before the weight
Of stones and hills of stones could break
Her down to mere quartz grit in that stony light
She turned back.

THE LADY AND THE
EARTHENWARE HEAD

Fired in sanguine clay, the model head
Fit nowhere: brickdust-complected, eye under
    a dense lid,
On the long bookshelf it stood
Stolidly propping thick volumes of prose: spite-set
    Ape of her look. Best rid
Hearthstone at once of the outrageous head;
Still, she felt loath to junk it.

No place, it seemed, for the effigy to fare
Free from all molesting. Rough boys,
    Spying a pate to spare
Glowering sullen and pompous from an ash-heap,
Might well seize this prize,
    Maltreat the hostage head in shocking wise,
And waken the sly nerve up

That knits to each original its coarse copy. A dark tarn
She thought of then, thick-silted, with weeds obscured,
    To serve her exacting turn:
But out of the watery aspic, laureled by fins,
    The simulacrum leered,
Lewdly beckoning, and her courage wavered:
She blenched, as one who drowns,

And resolved more ceremoniously to lodge
The mimic head – in a crotched willow, green-
Vaulted by foliage:
Let bell-tongued birds descant in blackest feather
On the rendering, grain by grain,
Of that uncouth shape to simple sod again
Through drear and dulcet weather.

Yet, shrined on her shelf, the grisly visage endured,
Despite her wrung hands, her tears, her praying:
     Vanish!
Steadfast and evil-starred,
It ogled through rock-fault, wind-flaw and fisted wave -
An antique hag-head, too tough for knife to finish,
Refusing to diminish
By one jot its basilisk-look of love.

ALL THE DEAD DEARS

In the Archaeological Museum in Cambridge
is a stone coffin of the fourth century A.D.
containing the skeletons of a woman, a mouse
and a shrew. The ankle-bone of the woman
has been slightly gnawn.

Rigged poker-stiff on her back
With a granite grin
This antique museum-cased lady
Lies, companioned by the gimcrack
Relics of a mouse and a shrew
That battened for a day on her ankle-bone.

These three, unmasked now, bear
Dry witness
To the gross eating game
We'd wink at if we didn't hear
Stars grinding, crumb by crumb,
Our own grist down to its bony face.

How they grip us through thin and thick,
These barnacle dead!
This lady here's no kin
Of mine, yet kin she is: she'll suck
Blood and whistle my marrow clean
To prove it. As I think now of her head,

From the mercury-backed glass
Mother, grandmother, greatgrandmother
Reach hag hands to haul me in,
And an image looms under the fishpond surface
Where the daft father went down
With orange duck-feet winnowing his hair –

All the long gone darlings: they
Get back, though, soon,
Soon: be it by wakes, weddings,
Childbirths or a family barbecue:
Any touch, taste, tang's
Fit for those outlaws to ride home on,

And to sanctuary: usurping the armchair
Between tick
And tack of the clock, until we go,
Each skulled-and-crossboned Gulliver
Riddled with ghosts, to lie
Deadlocked with them, taking root as cradles rock.

THE DISQUIETING MUSES

Mother, mother, what illbred aunt
Or what disfigured and unsightly
Cousin did you so unwisely keep
Unasked to my christening, that she
Sent these ladies in her stead
With heads like darning-eggs to nod
And nod and nod at foot and head
And at the left side of my crib?

Mother, who made to order stories
Of Mixie Blackshort the heroic bear,
Mother, whose witches always, always
Got baked into gingerbread, I wonder
Whether you saw them, whether you said
Words to rid me of those three ladies
Nodding by night around my bed,
Mouthless, eyeless, with stitched bald head.

In the hurricane, when father's twelve
Study windows bellied in
Like bubbles about to break, you fed
My brother and me cookies and Ovaltine
And helped the two of us to choir:
'Thor is angry: boom boom boom!
Thor is angry: we don't care!'
But those ladies broke the panes.

When on tiptoe the schoolgirls danced,
Blinking flashlights like fireflies
And singing the glowworm song, I could
Not lift a foot in the twinkle-dress
But, heavy-footed, stood aside
In the shadow cast by my dismal-headed
Godmothers, and you cried and cried:
And the shadow stretched, the lights went out.

Mother, you sent me to piano lessons
And praised my arabesques and trills
Although each teacher found my touch
Oddly wooden in spite of scales
And the hours of practicing, my ear
Tone-deaf and yes, unteachable.
I learned, I learned, I learned elsewhere,
From muses unhired by you, dear mother.

I woke one day to see you, mother,
Floating above me in bluest air
On a green balloon bright with a million
Flowers and bluebirds that never were
Never, never, found anywhere.
But the little planet bobbed away
Like a soap-bubble as you called: Come here!
And I faced my traveling companions.

Day now, night now, at head, side, feet,
They stand their vigil in gowns of stone,
Faces blank as the day I was born,
Their shadows long in the setting sun
That never brightens or goes down.
And this is the kingdom you bore me to,
Mother, mother. But no frown of mine
Will betray the company I keep.

OUIJA

It is a chilly god, a god of shades,
Rises to the glass from his black fathoms.
At the window, those unborn, those undone
Assemble with the frail paleness of moths,
An envious phosphorescence in their wings.
Vermilions, bronzes, colors of the sun
In the coal fire will not wholly console them.
Imagine their deep hunger, deep as the dark
For the blood-heat that would ruddle or reclaim.
The glass mouth sucks blood-heat from my forefinger.
The old god dribbles, in return, his words.

The old god, too, writes aureate poetry
In tarnished modes, maundering among the wastes,
Fair chronicler of every foul declension.
Age, and ages of prose, have uncoiled
His talking whirlwind, abated his excessive temper
When words, like locusts, drummed the darkening air
And left the cobs to rattle, bitten clean.
Skies once wearing a blue, divine hauteur
Ravel above us, mistily descend,
Thickening with motes, to a marriage with the mire.

He hymns the rotten queen with saffron hair
Who has saltier aphrodisiacs
Than virgins' tears. That bawdy queen of death,
Her wormy couriers are at his bones.
Still he hymns juice of her, hot nectarine.
I see him, horny-skinned and tough, construe
What flinty pebbles the ploughblade upturns
As ponderable tokens of her love.
He, godly, doddering, spells
No succinct Gabriel from the letters here
But floridly, his amorous nostalgias.

ON THE DECLINE OF ORACLES

My father kept a vaulted conch
By two bronze bookends of ships in sail,
And as I listened its cold teeth seethed
With voices of that ambiguous sea
Old Böcklin missed, who held a shell
To hear the sea he could not hear.
What the seashell spoke to his inner ear
He knew, but no peasants know.

My father died, and when he died
He willed his books and shell away.
The books burned up, sea took the shell,
But I, I keep the voices he
Set in my ear, and in my eye
The sight of those blue, unseen waves
For which the ghost of Böcklin grieves.
The peasants feast and multiply.

Eclipsing the spitted ox I see
Neither brazen swan nor burning star,
Heraldry of a starker age,
But three men entering the yard,
And those men coming up the stair.
Profitless, their gossiping images
Invade the cloistral eye like pages
From a gross comic strip, and toward

The happening of this happening
The earth turns now. In half an hour
I shall go down the shabby stair and meet,
Coming up, those three. Worth
Less than present, past – this future.
Worthless such vision to eyes gone dull
That once descried Troy's towers fall,
Saw evil break out of the north.

SNAKECHARMER

As the gods began one world, and man another,
So the snakecharmer begins a snaky sphere
With moon-eye, mouth-pipe. He pipes. Pipes green.
    Pipes water.

Pipes water green until green waters waver
With reedy lengths and necks and undulatings.
And as his notes twine green, the green river

Shapes its images around his songs.
He pipes a place to stand on, but no rocks,
No floor: a wave of flickering grass tongues

Supports his foot. He pipes a world of snakes,
Of sways and coilings, from the snake-rooted bottom
Of his mind. And now nothing but snakes

Is visible. The snake-scales have become
Leaf, become eyelid; snake-bodies, bough, breast
Of tree and human. And he within this snakedom

Rules the writhings which make manifest
His snakehood and his might with pliant tunes
From his thin pipe. Out of this green nest

As out of Eden's navel twist the lines
Of snaky generations: let there be snakes!
And snakes there were, are, will be – till yawns

Consume this piper and he tires of music
And pipes the world back to the simple fabric
Of snake-warp, snake-weft. Pipes the cloth of snakes

To a melting of green waters, till no snake
Shows its head, and those green waters back to
Water, to green, to nothing like a snake.
Puts up his pipe, and lids his moony eye.

1958

MUSSEL HUNTER AT
ROCK HARBOR

I came before the water-
Colorists came to get the
Good of the Cape light that scours
Sand grit to sided crystal
And buffs and sleeks the blunt hulls
Of the three fishing smacks beached
On the bank of the river's

Backtracking tail. I'd come for
Free fish-bait: the blue mussels
Clumped like bulbs at the grass-root
Margin of the tidal pools.
Dawn tide stood dead low. I smelt
Mud stench, shell guts, gulls' leavings;
Heard a queer crusty scrabble

Cease, and I neared the silenced
Edge of a cratered pool-bed
The mussels hung dull blue and
Conspicuous, yet it seemed
A sly world's hinges had swung
Shut against me. All held still.
Though I counted scant seconds,

Enough ages lapsed to win
Confidence of safe-conduct
In the wary otherworld
Eyeing me. Grass put forth claws;
Small mud knobs, nudged from under,
Displaced their domes as tiny
Knights might doff their casques. The crabs

Inched from their pigmy burrows
And from the trench-dug mud, all
Camouflaged in mottled mail
Of browns and greens. Each wore one
Claw swollen to a shield large
As itself – no fiddler's arm
Grown Gargantuan by trade,

But grown grimly, and grimly
Borne, for a use beyond my
Guessing of it. Sibilant
Mass-motived hordes, they sidled
Out in a converging stream
Toward the pool-mouth, perhaps to
Meet the thin and sluggish thread

Of sea retracing its tide-
Way up the river-basin.
Or to avoid me. They moved
Obliquely with a dry-wet

Sound, with a glittery wisp
And trickle. Could they feel mud
Pleasurable under claws

As I could between bare toes?
That question ended it – I
Stood shut out, for once, for all,
Puzzling the passage of their
Absolutely alien
Order as I might puzzle
At the clear tail of Halley's

Comet coolly giving my
Orbit the go-by, made known
By a family name it
Knew nothing of. So the crabs
Went about their business, which
Wasn't fiddling, and I filled
A big handkerchief with blue

Mussels. From what the crabs saw,
If they could see, I was one
Two-legged mussel-picker.
High on the airy thatching
Of the dense grasses I found
The husk of a fiddler-crab,
Intact, strangely strayed above

His world of mud – green color
And innards bleached and blown off
Somewhere by much sun and wind;
There was no telling if he'd
Died recluse or suicide
Or headstrong Columbus crab.
The crab-face, etched and set there,

Grimaced as skulls grimace: it
Had an Oriental look,
A samurai death mask done
On a tiger tooth, less for
Art's sake than God's. Far from sea –
Where red-freckled crab-backs, claws
And whole crabs, dead, their soggy

Bellies pallid and upturned,
Perform their shambling waltzes
On the waves' dissolving turn
And return, losing themselves
Bit by bit to their friendly
Element – this relic saved
Face, to face the bald-faced sun.

1959

THE BULL OF BENDYLAW

The black bull bellowed before the sea.
The sea, till that day orderly,
Hove up against Bendylaw.

The queen in the mulberry arbor stared
Stiff as a queen on a playing card.
The king fingered his beard.

A blue sea, four horny bull-feet,
A bull-snouted sea that wouldn't stay put,
Bucked at the garden gate.

Along box-lined walks in the florid sun
Toward the rowdy bellow and back again
The lords and ladies ran.

The great bronze gate began to crack,
The sea broke in at every crack,
Pellmell, blueblack.

The bull surged up, the bull surged down,
Not to be stayed by a daisy chain
Nor by any learned man.

O the king's tidy acre is under the sea,
And the royal rose in the bull's belly,
And the bull on the king's highway.

71

SUICIDE OFF EGG ROCK

Behind him the hotdogs split and drizzled
On the public grills, and the ochreous salt flats,
Gas tanks, factory stacks – that landscape
Of imperfections his bowels were part of –
Rippled and pulsed in the glassy updraught.
Sun struck the water like a damnation.
No pit of shadow to crawl into,
And his blood beating the old tattoo
I am, I am, I am. Children
Were squealing where combers broke and the spindrift
Raveled wind-ripped from the crest of the wave.
A mongrel working his legs to a gallop
Hustled a gull flock to flap off the sandspit.

He smoldered, as if stone-deaf, blindfold,
His body beached with the sea's garbage,
A machine to breathe and beat forever.
Flies filing in through a dead skate's eyehole
Buzzed and assailed the vaulted brainchamber.
The words in his book wormed off the pages.
Everything glittered like blank paper.

Everything shrank in the sun's corrosive
Ray but Egg Rock on the blue wastage.
He heard when he walked into the water

The forgetful surf creaming on those ledges.

METAPHORS

I'm a riddle in nine syllables,
An elephant, a ponderous house,
A melon strolling on two tendrils.
O red fruit, ivory, fine timbers!
This loaf's big with its yeasty rising.
Money's new-minted in this fat purse.
I'm a means, a stage, a cow in calf.
I've eaten a bag of green apples,
Boarded the train there's no getting off.

ELECTRA ON AZALEA PATH

The day you died I went into the dirt,
Into the lightless hibernaculum
Where bees, striped black and gold, sleep out the
      blizzard
Like hieratic stones, and the ground is hard.
It was good for twenty years, that wintering –
As if you had never existed, as if I came
God-fathered into the world from my mother's belly:
Her wide bed wore the stain of divinity.
I had nothing to do with guilt or anything
When I wormed back under my mother's heart.

Small as a doll in my dress of innocence
I lay dreaming your epic, image by image.
Nobody died or withered on that stage.
Everything took place in a durable whiteness.
The day I woke, I woke on Churchyard Hill.
I found your name, I found your bones and all
Enlisted in a cramped necropolis,
Your speckled stone askew by an iron fence.

In this charity ward, this poorhouse, where the dead
Crowd foot to foot, head to head, no flower
Breaks the soil. This is Azalea Path.
A field of burdock opens to the south.

Six feet of yellow gravel cover you.
The artificial red sage does not stir
In the basket of plastic evergreens they put
At the headstone next to yours, nor does it rot,
Although the rains dissolve a bloody dye:
The ersatz petals drip, and they drip red.

Another kind of redness bothers me:
The day your slack sail drank my sister's breath
The flat sea purpled like that evil cloth
My mother unrolled at your last homecoming.
I borrow the stilts of an old tragedy.
The truth is, one late October, at my birth-cry
A scorpion stung its head, an ill-starred thing;
My mother dreamed you face down in the sea.

The stony actors poise and pause for breath.
I brought my love to bear, and then you died.
It was the gangrene ate you to the bone
My mother said; you died like any man.
How shall I age into that state of mind?
I am the ghost of an infamous suicide,
My own blue razor rusting in my throat.
O pardon the one who knocks for pardon at
Your gate, father – your hound-bitch, daughter, friend.
It was my love that did us both to death.

THE BEEKEEPER'S DAUGHTER

A garden of mouthings. Purple, scarlet-speckled, black
The great corollas dilate, peeling back their silks.
Their musk encroaches, circle after circle,
A well of scents almost too dense to breathe in.
Hieratical in your frock coat, maestro of the bees,
You move among the many-breasted hives,

My heart under your foot, sister of a stone.

Trumpet-throats open to the beaks of birds.
The Golden Rain Tree drips its powders down.
In these little boudoirs streaked with orange and red
The anthers nod their heads, potent as kings
To father dynasties. The air is rich.
Here is a queenship no mother can contest –

A fruit that's death to taste: dark flesh, dark parings.

In burrows narrow as a finger, solitary bees
Keep house among the grasses. Kneeling down
I set my eye to a hole-mouth and meet an eye
Round, green, disconsolate as a tear.
Father, bridegroom, in this Easter egg
Under the coronal of sugar roses

The queen bee marries the winter of your year.

MAN IN BLACK

Where the three magenta
Breakwaters take the shove
And suck of the gray sea

To the left, and the wave
Unfists against the dun
Barb-wired headland of

The Deer Island prison
With its trim piggeries,
Hen huts and cattle green

To the right, and March ice
Glazes the rock pools yet,
Snuff-colored sand cliffs rise

Over a great stone spit
Bared by each falling tide,
And you, across those white

Stones, strode out in your dead
Black coat, black shoes, and your
Black hair till there you stood,

Fixed vortex on the far
Tip, riveting stones, air,
All of it, together.

THE COLOSSUS

I shall never get you put together entirely,
Pieced, glued, and properly jointed.
Mule-bray, pig-grunt and bawdy cackles
Proceed from your great lips.
It's worse than a barnyard.

Perhaps you consider yourself an oracle,
Mouthpiece of the dead, or of some god or other.
Thirty years now I have labored
To dredge the silt from your throat.
I am none the wiser.

Scaling little ladders with gluepots and pails of Lysol
I crawl like an ant in mourning
Over the weedy acres of your brow
To mend the immense skull-plates and clear
The bald, white tumuli of your eyes.

A blue sky out of the Oresteia
Arches above us. O father, all by yourself
You are pithy and historical as the Roman Forum.
I open my lunch on a hill of black cypress.
Your fluted bones and acanthine hair are littered

In their old anarchy to the horizon-line.
It would take more than a lightning-stroke
To create such a ruin.
Nights, I squat in the cornucopia
Of your left ear, out of the wind,

Counting the red stars and those of plum-color.
The sun rises under the pillar of your tongue.
My hours are married to shadow.
No longer do I listen for the scrape of a keel
On the blank stones of the landing.

POEM FOR A BIRTHDAY

1. Who

The month of flowering's finished. The fruit's in,
Eaten or rotten. I am all mouth.
October's the month for storage.

This shed's fusty as a mummy's stomach:
Old tools, handles and rusty tusks.
I am at home here among the dead heads.

Let me sit in a flowerpot,
The spiders won't notice.
My heart is a stopped geranium.

If only the wind would leave my lungs alone.
Dogbody noses the petals. They bloom upside down.
They rattle like hydrangea bushes.

Moldering heads console me,
Nailed to the rafters yesterday:
Inmates who don't hibernate.

Cabbageheads: wormy purple, silver-glaze,
A dressing of mule ears, mothy pelts, but
    green-hearted,
Their veins white as porkfat.

O the beauty of usage!
The orange pumpkins have no eyes.
These halls are full of women who think
   they are birds.

This is a dull school.
I am a root, a stone, an owl pellet,
Without dreams of any sort.

Mother, you are the one mouth
I would be a tongue to. Mother of otherness
Eat me. Wastebasket gaper, shadow of doorways.

I said: I must remember this, being small.
There were such enormous flowers,
Purple and red mouths, utterly lovely.

The hoops of blackberry stems made me cry.
Now they light me up like an electric bulb.
For weeks I can remember nothing at all.

2. Dark House
   This is a dark house, very big.
   I made it myself,
   Cell by cell from a quiet corner,
   Chewing at the gray paper,
   Oozing the glue drops,

Whistling, wiggling my ears,
Thinking of something else.

It has so many cellars,
Such eelish delvings!
I am round as an owl,
I see by my own light.
Any day I may litter puppies
Or mother a horse. My belly moves.
I must make more maps.

These marrowy tunnels!
Moley-handed, I eat my way.
All-mouth licks up the bushes
And the pots of meat.
He lives in an old well,
A stony hole. He's to blame.
He's a fat sort.

Pebble smells, turnipy chambers.
Small nostrils are breathing.
Little humble loves!
Footlings, boneless as noses,
It is warm and tolerable
In the bowel of the root.
Here's a cuddly mother.

3. *Maenad*

Once I was ordinary:
Sat by my father's bean tree
Eating the fingers of wisdom.
The birds made milk.
When it thundered I hid under a flat stone.

The mother of mouths didn't love me.
The old man shrank to a doll.
O I am too big to go backward:
Birdmilk is feathers,
The bean leaves are dumb as hands.

This month is fit for little.
The dead ripen in the grapeleaves.
A red tongue is among us.
Mother, keep out of my barnyard,
I am becoming another.

Dog-head, devourer:
Feed me the berries of dark.
The lids won't shut. Time
Unwinds from the great umbilicus of the sun
Its endless glitter.

I must swallow it all.

Lady, who are these others in the moon's vat –
Sleepdrunk, their limbs at odds?
In this light the blood is black.
Tell me my name.

4. *The Beast*

He was bullman earlier,
King of the dish, my lucky animal.
Breathing was easy in his airy holding.
The sun sat in his armpit.
Nothing went moldy. The little invisibles
Waited on him hand and foot.
The blue sisters sent me to another school.
Monkey lived under the dunce cap.
He kept blowing me kisses.
I hardly knew him.

He won't be got rid of:
Mumblepaws, teary and sorry,
Fido Littlesoul, the bowel's familiar.
A dustbin's enough for him.
The dark's his bone.
Call him any name, he'll come to it.

Mud-sump, happy sty-face.
I've married a cupboard of rubbish.
I bed in a fish puddle.

Down here the sky is always falling.
Hogwallow's at the window.
The star bugs won't save me this month.
I housekeep in Time's gut-end
Among emmets and mollusks,
Duchess of Nothing,
Hairtusk's bride.

5. *Flute Notes from a Reedy Pond*

Now coldness comes sifting down, layer after layer,
To our bower at the lily root.
Overhead the old umbrellas of summer
Wither like pithless hands. There is little shelter.

Hourly the eye of the sky enlarges its blank
Dominion. The stars are no nearer.
Already frog-mouth and fish-mouth drink
The liquor of indolence, and all things sink

Into a soft caul of forgetfulness.
The fugitive colors die.
Caddis worms drowse in their silk cases,
The lamp-headed nymphs are nodding to sleep
    like statues.

Puppets, loosed from the strings of the puppet-master,
Wear masks of horn to bed.

This is not death, it is something safer.
The wingy myths won't tug at us any more:

The molts are tongueless that sang from above
    the water
Of golgotha at the tip of a reed,
And how a god flimsy as a baby's finger
Shall unhusk himself and steer into the air.

6. *Witch Burning*
In the marketplace they are piling the dry sticks.
A thicket of shadows is a poor coat. I inhabit
The wax image of myself, a doll's body.
Sickness begins here: I am a dartboard for witches.
Only the devil can eat the devil out.
In the month of red leaves I climb to a bed of fire.

It is easy to blame the dark: the mouth of a door,
The cellar's belly. They've blown my sparkler out.
A black-sharded lady keeps me in a parrot cage.
What large eyes the dead have!
I am intimate with a hairy spirit.
Smoke wheels from the beak of this empty jar.

If I am a little one, I can do no harm.
If I don't move about, I'll knock nothing over. So I said,
Sitting under a potlid, tiny and inert as a rice grain.

They are turning the burners up, ring after ring.
We are full of starch, my small white fellows. We grow.
It hurts at first. The red tongues will teach the truth.

Mother of beetles, only unclench your hand:
I'll fly through the candle's mouth like a singeless moth.
Give me back my shape. I am ready to construe the days
I coupled with dust in the shadow of a stone.
My ankles brighten. Brightness ascends my thighs.
I am lost, I am lost, in the robes of all this light.

7. *The Stones*

This is the city where men are mended.
I lie on a great anvil.
The flat blue sky-circle

Flew off like the hat of a doll
When I fell out of the light. I entered
The stomach of indifference, the wordless cupboard.

The mother of pestles diminished me.
I became a still pebble.
The stones of the belly were peaceable,

The head-stone quiet, jostled by nothing.
Only the mouth-hole piped out,
Importunate cricket

In a quarry of silences.
The people of the city heard it.
They hunted the stones, taciturn and separate,

The mouth-hole crying their locations.
Drunk as a foetus
I suck at the paps of darkness.

The food tubes embrace me. Sponges kiss my
    lichens away.
The jewelmaster drives his chisel to pry
Open one stone eye.

This is the after-hell: I see the light.
A wind unstoppers the chamber
Of the ear, old worrier.

Water mollifies the flint lip,
And daylight lays its sameness on the wall.
The grafters are cheerful,

Heating the pincers, hoisting the delicate hammers.
A current agitates the wires
Volt upon volt. Catgut stitches my fissures.

A workman walks by carrying a pink torso.
The storerooms are full of hearts.
This is the city of spare parts.

My swaddled legs and arms smell sweet as rubber.
Here they can doctor heads, or any limb.
On Fridays the little children come

To trade their hooks for hands.
Dead men leave eyes for others.
Love is the uniform of my bald nurse.

Love is the bone and sinew of my curse.
The vase, reconstructed, houses
The elusive rose.

Ten fingers shape a bowl for shadows.
My mendings itch. There is nothing to do.
I shall be good as new.

MUSHROOMS

Overnight, very
Whitely, discreetly,
Very quietly

Our toes, our noses
Take hold on the loam,
Acquire the air.

Nobody sees us,
Stops us, betrays us;
The small grains make room.

Soft fists insist on
Heaving the needles,
The leafy bedding,

Even the paving.
Our hammers, our rams,
Earless and eyeless,

Perfectly voiceless,
Widen the crannies,
Shoulder through holes. We

Diet on water,
On crumbs of shadow,
Bland-mannered, asking

Little or nothing.
So many of us!
So many of us!

We are shelves, we are
Tables, we are meek,
We are edible,

Nudgers and shovers
In spite of ourselves.
Our kind multiplies:

We shall by morning
Inherit the earth.
Our foot's in the door.

1960

YOU'RE

Clownlike, happiest on your hands,
Feet to the stars, and moon-skulled,
Gilled like a fish. A common-sense
Thumbs-down on the dodo's mode.
Wrapped up in yourself like a spool,
Trawling your dark as owls do.
Mute as a turnip from the Fourth
Of July to All Fools' Day,
O high-riser, my little loaf.

Vague as fog and looked for like mail.
Farther off than Australia.
Bent-backed Atlas, our traveled prawn.
Snug as a bud and at home
Like a sprat in a pickle jug.
A creel of eels, all ripples.
Jumpy as a Mexican bean.
Right, like a well-done sum.
A clean slate, with your own face on.

THE HANGING MAN

By the roots of my hair some god got hold of me.
I sizzled in his blue volts like a desert prophet.

The nights snapped out of sight like a lizard's eyelid:
A world of bald white days in a shadeless socket.

A vulturous boredom pinned me in this tree.
If he were I, he would do what I did.

STILLBORN

These poems do not live: it's a sad diagnosis.
They grew their toes and fingers well enough,
Their little foreheads bulged with concentration.
If they missed out on walking about like people
It wasn't for any lack of mother-love.

O I cannot understand what happened to them!
They are proper in shape and number and every part.
They sit so nicely in the pickling fluid!
They smile and smile and smile and smile at me.
And still the lungs won't fill and the heart won't start.

They are not pigs, they are not even fish,
Though they have a piggy and a fishy air –
It would be better if they were alive, and that's
        what they were.
But they are dead, and their mother near dead
        with distraction,
And they stupidly stare, and do not speak of her.

CANDLES

They are the last romantics, these candles:
Upside down hearts of light tipping wax fingers,
And the fingers, taken in by their own haloes,
Grown milky, almost clear, like the bodies of saints.
It is touching, the way they'll ignore

A whole family of prominent objects
Simply to plumb the deeps of an eye
In its hollow of shadows, its fringe of reeds,
And the owner past thirty, no beauty at all.
Daylight would be more judicious,

Giving everybody a fair hearing.
They should have gone out with balloon flights
    and the stereopticon.
This is no time for the private point of view.
When I light them, my nostrils prickle.
Their pale, tentative yellows

Drag up false, Edwardian sentiments,
And I remember my maternal grandmother from Vienna.
As a schoolgirl she gave roses to Franz Josef.
The burghers sweated and wept. The children
    wore white.
And my grandfather moped in the Tyrol,

Imagining himself a headwaiter in America,
Floating in a high-church hush
Among ice buckets, frosty napkins.
These little globes of light are sweet as pears.
Kindly with invalids and mawkish women,

They mollify the bald moon.
Nun-souled, they burn heavenward and never marry.
The eyes of the child I nurse are scarcely open.
In twenty years I shall be retrograde
As these draughty ephemerids.

I watch their spilt tears cloud and dull to pearls.
How shall I tell anything at all
To this infant still in a birth-drowse?
Tonight, like a shawl, the mild light enfolds her,
The shadows stoop over like guests at a christening.

1961

ZOO KEEPER'S WIFE

I can stay awake all night, if need be –
Cold as an eel, without eyelids.
Like a dead lake the dark envelops me,
Blueblack, a spectacular plum fruit.
No airbubbles start from my heart, I am lungless
And ugly, my belly a silk stocking
Where the heads and tails of my sisters decompose.
Look, they are melting like coins in the powerful juices –

The spidery jaws, the spine bones bared for a moment
Like the white lines on a blueprint.
Should I stir, I think this pink and purple plastic
Guts bag would clack like a child's rattle,
Old grievances jostling each other, so many
        loose teeth.
But what do you know about that
My fat pork, my marrowy sweetheart, face-to-
        the-wall?
Some things of this world are indigestible.

You wooed me with the wolf-headed fruit bats
Hanging from their scorched hooks in the moist
Fug of the Small Mammal House.
The armadillo dozed in his sandbin
Obscene and bald as a pig, the white mice

Multiplied to infinity like angels on a pinhead
Out of sheer boredom. Tangled in the sweat-wet sheets
I remember the bloodied chicks and the quartered
        rabbits.

You checked the diet charts and took me to play
With the boa constrictor in the Fellows' Garden.
I pretended I was the Tree of Knowledge.
I entered your bible, I boarded your ark
With the sacred baboon in his wig and wax ears
And the bear-furred, bird-eating spider
Clambering round its glass box like an
        eight-fingered hand.
I can't get it out of my mind

How our courtship lit the tindery cages –
Your two-horned rhinoceros opened a mouth
Dirty as a bootsole and big as a hospital sink
For my cube of sugar: its bog breath
Gloved my arm to the elbow.
The snails blew kisses like black apples.
Nightly now I flog apes owls bears sheep
Over their iron stile. And still don't sleep.

FACE LIFT

You bring me good news from the clinic,
Whipping off your silk scarf, exhibiting the tight white
Mummy-cloths, smiling: I'm all right.
When I was nine, a lime-green anesthetist
Fed me banana gas through a frog-mask.
         The nauseous vault
Boomed with bad dreams and the Jovian voices
         of surgeons.
Then mother swam up, holding a tin basin.
O I was sick.

They've changed all that. Traveling
Nude as Cleopatra in my well-boiled hospital shift,
Fizzy with sedatives and unusually humorous,
I roll to an anteroom where a kind man
Fists my fingers for me. He makes me feel something
         precious
Is leaking from the finger-vents. At the count of two
Darkness wipes me out like chalk on a blackboard . . .
I don't know a thing.

For five days I lie in secret,
Tapped like a cask, the years draining into my pillow.
Even my best friend thinks I'm in the country.
Skin doesn't have roots, it peels away easy as paper.

When I grin, the stitches tauten. I grow backward.
 I'm twenty,
Broody and in long skirts on my first husband's sofa,
 my fingers
Buried in the lambswool of the dead poodle;
I hadn't a cat yet.

Now she's done for, the dewlapped lady
I watched settle, line by line, in my mirror –
Old sock-face, sagged on a darning egg.
They've trapped her in some laboratory jar.
Let her die there, or wither incessantly for the next
 fifty years,
Nodding and rocking and fingering her thin hair.
Mother to myself, I wake swaddled in gauze,
Pink and smooth as a baby.

MORNING SONG

Love set you going like a fat gold watch.
The midwife slapped your footsoles, and your bald cry
Took its place among the elements.

Our voices echo, magnifying your arrival. New statue.
In a drafty museum, your nakedness
Shadows our safety. We stand round blankly as walls.

I'm no more your mother
Than the cloud that distills a mirror to reflect its
    own slow
Effacement at the wind's hand.

All night your moth-breath
Flickers among the flat pink roses. I wake to listen:
A far sea moves in my ear.

One cry, and I stumble from bed, cow-heavy and floral
In my Victorian nightgown.
Your mouth opens clean as a cat's. The window square

Whitens and swallows its dull stars. And now you try
Your handful of notes;
The clear vowels rise like balloons.

BARREN WOMAN

Empty, I echo to the least footfall,
Museum without statues, grand with pillars, porticoes,
    rotundas.
In my courtyard a fountain leaps and sinks back
    into itself,
Nun-hearted and blind to the world. Marble lilies
Exhale their pallor like scent.

I imagine myself with a great public,
Mother of a white Nike and several bald-eyed Apollos.
Instead, the dead injure me with attentions,
    and nothing can happen.
The moon lays a hand on my forehead,
Blank-faced and mum as a nurse.

HEAVY WOMEN

Irrefutable, beautifully smug
As Venus, pedestaled on a half-shell
Shawled in blond hair and the salt
Scrim of a sea breeze, the women
Settle in their belling dresses.
Over each weighty stomach a face
Floats calm as a moon or a cloud.

Smiling to themselves, they meditate
Devoutly as the Dutch bulb
Forming its twenty petals.
The dark still nurses its secret.
On the green hill, under the thorn trees,
They listen for the millennium,
The knock of the small, new heart.

Pink-buttocked infants attend them.
Looping wool, doing nothing in particular,
They step among the archetypes.
Dusk hoods them in Mary-blue
While far off, the axle of winter
Grinds round, bearing down with the straw,
The star, the wise gray men.

IN PLASTER

I shall never get out of this! There are two of me now:
This new absolutely white person and the old
    yellow one,
And the white person is certainly the superior one.
She doesn't need food, she is one of the real saints.
At the beginning I hated her, she had no personality –
She lay in bed with me like a dead body
And I was scared, because she was shaped just the
    way I was

Only much whiter and unbreakable and with no
    complaints.
I couldn't sleep for a week, she was so cold.
I blamed her for everything, but she didn't answer.
I couldn't understand her stupid behavior!
When I hit her she held still, like a true pacifist.
Then I realized what she wanted was for me to
    love her:
She began to warm up, and I saw her advantages.

Without me, she wouldn't exist, so of course she
    was grateful.
I gave her a soul, I bloomed out of her as a rose
Blooms out of a vase of not very valuable porcelain,
And it was I who attracted everybody's attention,

Not her whiteness and beauty, as I had at first supposed.
I patronized her a little, and she lapped it up –
You could tell almost at once she had a slave mentality.

I didn't mind her waiting on me, and she adored it.
In the morning she woke me early, reflecting the sun
From her amazingly white torso, and I couldn't help
    but notice
Her tidiness and her calmness and her patience:
She humored my weakness like the best of nurses,
Holding my bones in place so they would mend
    properly.
In time our relationship grew more intense.

She stopped fitting me so closely and seemed offish.
I felt her criticizing me in spite of herself,
As if my habits offended her in some way.
She let in the drafts and became more and more
    absent-minded.
And my skin itched and flaked away in soft pieces
Simply because she looked after me so badly.
Then I saw what the trouble was: she thought she
    was immortal.

She wanted to leave me, she thought she was superior,
And I'd been keeping her in the dark, and she was
    resentful –

Wasting her days waiting on a half-corpse!
And secretly she began to hope I'd die.
Then she could cover my mouth and eyes, cover
    me entirely,
And wear my painted face the way a mummy-case
Wears the face of a pharaoh, though it's made of mud
    and water.

I wasn't in any position to get rid of her.
She'd supported me for so long I was quite limp –
I had even forgotten how to walk or sit,
So I was careful not to upset her in any way
Or brag ahead of time how I'd avenge myself.
Living with her was like living with my own coffin:
Yet I still depended on her, though I did it regretfully.

I used to think we might make a go of it together –
After all, it was a kind of marriage, being so close.
Now I see it must be one or the other of us.
She may be a saint, and I may be ugly and hairy,
But she'll soon find out that that doesn't matter a bit.
I'm collecting my strength; one day I shall manage
    without her,
And she'll perish with emptiness then, and begin to
    miss me.

TULIPS

The tulips are too excitable, it is winter here.
Look how white everything is, how quiet, how
         snowed-in.
I am learning peacefulness, lying by myself quietly
As the light lies on these white walls, this bed,
         these hands.
I am nobody; I have nothing to do with explosions.
I have given my name and my day-clothes up to
         the nurses
And my history to the anesthetist and my body
         to surgeons.

They have propped my head between the pillow and
         the sheet-cuff
Like an eye between two white lids that will not shut.
Stupid pupil, it has to take everything in.
The nurses pass and pass, they are no trouble,
They pass the way gulls pass inland in their white caps,
Doing things with their hands, one just the same
         as another,
So it is impossible to tell how many there are.

My body is a pebble to them, they tend it as water
Tends to the pebbles it must run over, smoothing
         them gently.

They bring me numbness in their bright needles, they
    bring me sleep.
Now I have lost myself I am sick of baggage—
My patent leather overnight case like a black pillbox,
My husband and child smiling out of the family photo;
Their smiles catch onto my skin, little smiling hooks.

I have let things slip, a thirty-year-old cargo boat
Stubbornly hanging on to my name and address.
They have swabbed me clear of my loving associations.
Scared and bare on the green plastic-pillowed trolley
I watched my teaset, my bureaus of linen, my books
Sink out of sight, and the water went over my head.
I am a nun now, I have never been so pure.

I didn't want any flowers, I only wanted
To lie with my hands turned up and be utterly empty.
How free it is, you have no idea how free—
The peacefulness is so big it dazes you,
And it asks nothing, a name tag, a few trinkets.
It is what the dead close on, finally; I imagine them
Shutting their mouths on it, like a Communion tablet.

The tulips are too red in the first place, they hurt me.
Even through the gift paper I could hear them breathe
Lightly, through their white swaddlings, like an
    awful baby.

Their redness talks to my wound, it corresponds.
They are subtle: they seem to float, though they weigh
    me down,
Upsetting me with their sudden tongues and their color,
A dozen red lead sinkers round my neck.

Nobody watched me before, now I am watched.
The tulips turn to me, and the window behind me
Where once a day the light slowly widens and
    slowly thins,
And I see myself, flat, ridiculous, a cut-paper shadow
Between the eye of the sun and the eyes of the tulips,
And I have no face, I have wanted to efface myself.
The vivid tulips eat my oxygen.

Before they came the air was calm enough,
Coming and going, breath by breath, without any fuss.
Then the tulips filled it up like a loud noise.
Now the air snags and eddies round them the way
    a river
Snags and eddies round a sunken rust-red engine.
They concentrate my attention, that was happy
Playing and resting without committing itself.

The walls, also, seem to be warming themselves.
The tulips should be behind bars like dangerous
    animals;

They are opening like the mouth of some great
        African cat,
And I am aware of my heart: it opens and closes
Its bowl of red blooms out of sheer love of me.
The water I taste is warm and salt, like the sea,
And comes from a country far away as health.

I AM VERTICAL

But I would rather be horizontal.
I am not a tree with my root in the soil
Sucking up minerals and motherly love
So that each March I may gleam into leaf,
Nor am I the beauty of a garden bed
Attracting my share of Ahs and spectacularly painted,
Unknowing I must soon unpetal.
Compared with me, a tree is immortal
And a flower-head not tall, but more startling,
And I want the one's longevity and the other's daring.

Tonight, in the infinitesimal light of the stars,
The trees and flowers have been strewing their
      cool odors.
I walk among them, but none of them are noticing.
Sometimes I think that when I am sleeping
I must most perfectly resemble them –
Thoughts gone dim.
It is more natural to me, lying down.
Then the sky and I are in open conversation,
And I shall be useful when I lie down finally:
Then the trees may touch me for once, and the flowers
      have time for me.

BLACKBERRYING

Nobody in the lane, and nothing, nothing but
    blackberries,
Blackberries on either side, though on the right mainly,
A blackberry alley, going down in hooks, and a sea
Somewhere at the end of it, heaving. Blackberries
Big as the ball of my thumb, and dumb as eyes
Ebon in the hedges, fat
With blue-red juices. These they squander on my fingers.
I had not asked for such a blood sisterhood; they must
    love me.
They accommodate themselves to my milkbottle,
    flattening their sides.

Overhead go the choughs in black, cacophonous flocks –
Bits of burnt paper wheeling in a blown sky.
Theirs is the only voice, protesting, protesting.
I do not think the sea will appear at all.
The high, green meadows are glowing, as if lit
    from within.
I come to one bush of berries so ripe it is a bush of flies,
Hanging their bluegreen bellies and their wing panes
    in a Chinese screen.
The honey-feast of the berries has stunned them; they
    believe in heaven.
One more hook, and the berries and bushes end.

The only thing to come now is the sea.
From between two hills a sudden wind funnels at me,
Slapping its phantom laundry in my face.
These hills are too green and sweet to have tasted salt.
I follow the sheep path between them. A last hook
        brings me
To the hills' northern face, and the face is orange rock
That looks out on nothing, nothing but a great space
Of white and pewter lights, and a din like silversmiths
Beating and beating at an intractable metal.

THE MOON AND THE YEW TREE

This is the light of the mind, cold and planetary.
The trees of the mind are black. The light is blue.
The grasses unload their griefs on my feet as if
    I were God,
Prickling my ankles and murmuring of their humility.
Fumy, spiritous mists inhabit this place
Separated from my house by a row of headstones.
I simply cannot see where there is to get to.

The moon is no door. It is a face in its own right,
White as a knuckle and terribly upset.
It drags the sea after it like a dark crime; it is quiet
With the O-gape of complete despair. I live here.
Twice on Sunday, the bells startle the sky—
Eight great tongues affirming the Resurrection.
At the end, they soberly bong out their names.

The yew tree points up. It has a Gothic shape.
The eyes lift after it and find the moon.
The moon is my mother. She is not sweet like Mary.
Her blue garments unloose small bats and owls.
How I would like to believe in tenderness—
The face of the effigy, gentled by candles,
Bending, on me in particular, its mild eyes.

I have fallen a long way. Clouds are flowering
Blue and mystical over the face of the stars.
Inside the church, the saints will be all blue,
Floating on their delicate feet over the cold pews,
Their hands and faces stiff with holiness.
The moon sees nothing of this. She is bald and wild.
And the message of the yew tree is blackness –
   blackness and silence.

MIRROR

I am silver and exact. I have no preconceptions.
Whatever I see I swallow immediately
Just as it is, unmisted by love or dislike.
I am not cruel, only truthful –
The eye of a little god, four-cornered.
Most of the time I meditate on the opposite wall.
It is pink, with speckles. I have looked at it so long
I think it is a part of my heart. But it flickers.
Faces and darkness separate us over and over.

Now I am a lake. A woman bends over me,
Searching my reaches for what she really is.
Then she turns to those liars, the candles or the moon.
I see her back, and reflect it faithfully.
She rewards me with tears and an agitation of hands.
I am important to her. She comes and goes.
Each morning it is her face that replaces the darkness.
In me she has drowned a young girl, and in me an
      old woman
Rises toward her day after day, like a terrible fish.

1962

THREE WOMEN

A POEM FOR THREE VOICES
Setting: A Maternity Ward and round about

FIRST VOICE:
I am slow as the world. I am very patient,
Turning through my time, the suns and stars
Regarding me with attention.
The moon's concern is more personal:
She passes and repasses, luminous as a nurse.
Is she sorry for what will happen? I do not think so.
She is simply astonished at fertility.

When I walk out, I am a great event.
I do not have to think, or even rehearse.
What happens in me will happen without attention.
The pheasant stands on the hill;
He is arranging his brown feathers.
I cannot help smiling at what it is I know.
Leaves and petals attend me. I am ready.

SECOND VOICE:
When I first saw it, the small red seep, I did not believe it.
I watched the men walk about me in the office. They
        were so flat!
There was something about them like cardboard, and
        now I had caught it,

That flat, flat, flatness from which ideas, destructions,
Bulldozers, guillotines, white chambers of shrieks
    proceed,
Endlessly proceed – and the cold angels,
    the abstractions.
I sat at my desk in my stockings, my high heels,

And the man I work for laughed: 'Have you seen
    something awful?
You are so white, suddenly.' And I said nothing.
I saw death in the bare trees, a deprivation.
I could not believe it. Is it so difficult
For the spirit to conceive a face, a mouth?
The letters proceed from these black keys, and these
    black keys proceed
From my alphabetical fingers, ordering parts,

Parts, bits, cogs, the shining multiples.
I am dying as I sit. I lose a dimension.
Trains roar in my ears, departures, departures!
The silver track of time empties into the distance,
The white sky empties of its promise, like a cup.
These are my feet, these mechanical echoes.
Tap, tap, tap, steel pegs. I am found wanting.

This is a disease I carry home, this is a death.
Again, this is a death. Is it the air,

The particles of destruction I suck up? Am I a pulse
That wanes and wanes, facing the cold angel?
Is this my lover then? This death, this death?
As a child I loved a lichen-bitten name.
Is this the one sin then, this old dead love of death?

THIRD VOICE:
I remember the minute when I knew for sure.
The willows were chilling,
The face in the pool was beautiful, but not mine –
It had a consequential look, like everything else,
And all I could see was dangers: doves and words,
Stars and showers of gold – conceptions, conceptions!
I remember a white, cold wing

And the great swan, with its terrible look,
Coming at me, like a castle, from the top of the river.
There is a snake in swans.
He glided by; his eye had a black meaning.
I saw the world in it – small, mean and black,
Every little word hooked to every little word,
        and act to act.
A hot blue day had budded into something.

I wasn't ready. The white clouds rearing
Aside were dragging me in four directions.
I wasn't ready.

I had no reverence.
I thought I could deny the consequence –
But it was too late for that. It was too late, and the face
Went on shaping itself with love, as if I was ready.

SECOND VOICE:
It is a world of snow now. I am not at home.
How white these sheets are. The faces have no features.
They are bald and impossible, like the faces of
    my children,
Those little sick ones that elude my arms.
Other children do not touch me: they are terrible.
They have too many colors, too much life. They are
    not quiet,
Quiet, like the little emptinesses I carry.

I have had my chances. I have tried and tried.
I have stitched life into me like a rare organ,
And walked carefully, precariously, like
    something rare.
I have tried not to think too hard. I have tried
    to be natural.
I have tried to be blind in love, like other women,
Blind in my bed, with my dear blind sweet one,
Not looking, through the thick dark, for the face
    of another.

I did not look. But still the face was there,
The face of the unborn one that loved its perfections,
The face of the dead one that could only be perfect
In its easy peace, could only keep holy so.
And then there were other faces. The faces of nations,
Governments, parliaments, societies,
The faceless faces of important men.

It is these men I mind:
They are so jealous of anything that is not flat!
    They are jealous gods
That would have the whole world flat because they are.
I see the Father conversing with the Son.
Such flatness cannot but be holy.
'Let us make a heaven,' they say.
'Let us flatten and launder the grossness from
    these souls.'

FIRST VOICE:
I am calm. I am calm. It is the calm before something
    awful:
The yellow minute before the wind walks, when
    the leaves
Turn up their hands, their pallors. It is so quiet here.
The sheets, the faces, are white and stopped,
    like clocks.
Voices stand back and flatten. Their visible hieroglyphs

Flatten to parchment screens to keep the wind off.
They paint such secrets in Arabic, Chinese!

I am dumb and brown. I am a seed about to break.
The brownness is my dead self, and it is sullen:
It does not wish to be more, or different.
Dusk hoods me in blue now, like a Mary.
O color of distance and forgetfulness! –
When will it be, the second when Time breaks
And eternity engulfs it, and I drown utterly?

I talk to myself, myself only, set apart –
Swabbed and lurid with disinfectants, sacrificial.
Waiting lies heavy on my lids. It lies like sleep,
Like a big sea. Far off, far off, I feel the first wave tug
Its cargo of agony toward me, inescapable, tidal.
And I, a shell, echoing on this white beach
Face the voices that overwhelm, the terrible element.

THIRD VOICE:
I am a mountain now, among mountainy women.
The doctors move among us as if our bigness
Frightened the mind. They smile like fools.
They are to blame for what I am, and they know it.
They hug their flatness like a kind of health.
And what if they found themselves surprised, as I did?
They would go mad with it.

And what if two lives leaked between my thighs?
I have seen the white clean chamber with its instruments.
It is a place of shrieks. It is not happy.
'This is where you will come when you are ready.'
The night lights are flat red moons. They are dull
    with blood.
I am not ready for anything to happen.
I should have murdered this, that murders me.

FIRST VOICE:
There is no miracle more cruel than this.
I am dragged by the horses, the iron hooves.
I last. I last it out. I accomplish a work.
Dark tunnel, through which hurtle the visitations,
The visitations, the manifestations, the startled faces.
I am the center of an atrocity.
What pains, what sorrows must I be mothering?

Can such innocence kill and kill? It milks my life.
The trees wither in the street. The rain is corrosive.
I taste it on my tongue, and the workable horrors,
The horrors that stand and idle, the slighted
    godmothers
With their hearts that tick and tick, with their satchels
    of instruments.
I shall be a wall and a roof, protecting.
I shall be a sky and a hill of good: O let me be!

A power is growing on me, an old tenacity.
I am breaking apart like the world. There is this
    blackness,
This ram of blackness. I fold my hands on a mountain.
The air is thick. It is thick with this working.
I am used. I am drummed into use.
My eyes are squeezed by this blackness.
I see nothing.

SECOND VOICE:
I am accused. I dream of massacres.
I am a garden of black and red agonies. I drink them,
Hating myself, hating and fearing. And now the
    world conceives
Its end and runs toward it, arms held out in love.
It is a love of death that sickens everything.
A dead sun stains the newsprint. It is red.
I lose life after life. The dark earth drinks them.

She is the vampire of us all. So she supports us,
Fattens us, is kind. Her mouth is red.
I know her. I know her intimately –
Old winter-face, old barren one, old time bomb.
Men have used her meanly. She will eat them.
Eat them, eat them, eat them in the end.
The sun is down. I die. I make a death.

Who is he, this blue, furious boy,
Shiny and strange, as if he had hurtled from a star?
He is looking so angrily!
He flew into the room, a shriek at his heel.
The blue color pales. He is human after all.
A red lotus opens in its bowl of blood;
They are stitching me up with silk, as if I were
      a material.

What did my fingers do before they held him?
What did my heart do, with its love?
I have never seen a thing so clear.
His lids are like the lilac-flower
And soft as a moth, his breath.
I shall not let go.
There is no guile or warp in him. May he keep so.

SECOND VOICE:
There is the moon in the high window. It is over.
How winter fills my soul! And that chalk light
Laying its scales on the windows, the windows of
      empty offices,
Empty schoolrooms, empty churches. O so much
      emptiness!
There is this cessation. This terrible cessation
      of everything.

These bodies mounded around me now, these polar
        sleepers –
What blue, moony ray ices their dreams?

I feel it enter me, cold, alien, like an instrument.
And that mad, hard face at the end of it, that O-mouth
Open in its gape of perpetual grieving.
It is she that drags the blood-black sea around
Month after month, with its voices of failure.
I am helpless as the sea at the end of her string.
I am restless. Restless and useless. I, too, create corpses.

I shall move north. I shall move into a long blackness.
I see myself as a shadow, neither man nor woman,
Neither a woman, happy to be like a man, nor a man
Blunt and flat enough to feel no lack. I feel a lack.
I hold my fingers up, ten white pickets.
See, the darkness is leaking from the cracks.
I cannot contain it. I cannot contain my life.

I shall be a heroine of the peripheral.
I shall not be accused by isolate buttons,
Holes in the heels of socks, the white mute faces
Of unanswered letters, coffined in a letter case.
I shall not be accused, I shall not be accused.
The clock shall not find me wanting, nor these stars
That rivet in place abyss after abyss.

THIRD VOICE:
I see her in my sleep, my red, terrible girl.
She is crying through the glass that separates us.
She is crying, and she is furious.
Her cries are hooks that catch and grate like cats.
It is by these hooks she climbs to my notice.
She is crying at the dark, or at the stars
That at such a distance from us shine and whirl.

I think her little head is carved in wood,
A red, hard wood, eyes shut and mouth wide open.
And from the open mouth issue sharp cries
Scratching at my sleep like arrows,
Scratching at my sleep, and entering my side.
My daughter has no teeth. Her mouth is wide.
It utters such dark sounds it cannot be good.

FIRST VOICE:
What is it that flings these innocent souls at us?
Look, they are so exhausted, they are all flat out
In their canvas-sided cots, names tied to their wrists,
The little silver trophies they've come so far for.
There are some with thick black hair, there are
        some bald.
Their skin tints are pink or sallow, brown or red;
They are beginning to remember their differences.

I think they are made of water; they have no
    expression.
Their features are sleeping, like light on quiet water.
They are the real monks and nuns in their identical
    garments.
I see them showering like stars on to the world –
On India, Africa, America, these miraculous ones,
These pure, small images. They smell of milk.
Their footsoles are untouched. They are walkers of air.

Can nothingness be so prodigal?
Here is my son.
His wide eye is that general, flat blue.
He is turning to me like a little, blind, bright plant.
One cry. It is the hook I hang on.
And I am a river of milk.
I am a warm hill.

SECOND VOICE:
I am not ugly. I am even beautiful.
The mirror gives back a woman without deformity.
The nurses give back my clothes, and an identity.
It is usual, they say, for such a thing to happen.
It is usual in my life, and the lives of others.
I am one in five, something like that. I am not hopeless.
I am beautiful as a statistic. Here is my lipstick.

I draw on the old mouth.
The red mouth I put by with my identity
A day ago, two days, three days ago. It was
    a Friday.
I do not even need a holiday; I can go to work today.
I can love my husband, who will understand.
Who will love me through the blur of my deformity
As if I had lost an eye, a leg, a tongue.

And so I stand, a little sightless. So I walk
Away on wheels, instead of legs, they serve as well.
And learn to speak with fingers, not a tongue.
The body is resourceful.
The body of a starfish can grow back its arms
And newts are prodigal in legs. And may I be
As prodigal in what lacks me.

THIRD VOICE:
She is a small island, asleep and peaceful,
And I am a white ship hooting: Goodbye, goodbye.
The day is blazing. It is very mournful.
The flowers in this room are red and tropical.
They have lived behind glass all their lives, they have
    been cared for tenderly.
Now they face a winter of white sheets, white faces.
There is very little to go into my suitcase.

There are the clothes of a fat woman I do not know.
There is my comb and brush. There is an emptiness.
I am so vulnerable suddenly.
I am a wound walking out of hospital.
I am a wound that they are letting go.
I leave my health behind. I leave someone
Who would adhere to me: I undo her fingers like
    bandages: I go.

SECOND VOICE:
I am myself again. There are no loose ends.
I am bled white as wax, I have no attachments.
I am flat and virginal, which means nothing has
    happened,
Nothing that cannot be erased, ripped up and scrapped,
    begun again.
These little black twigs do not think to bud,
Nor do these dry, dry gutters dream of rain.
This woman who meets me in windows – she is neat.

So neat she is transparent, like a spirit.
How shyly she superimposes her neat self
On the inferno of African oranges, the heel-hung pigs.
She is deferring to reality.
It is I. It is I –
Tasting the bitterness between my teeth.
The incalculable malice of the everyday.

FIRST VOICE:
How long can I be a wall, keeping the wind off?
How long can I be
Gentling the sun with the shade of my hand,
Intercepting the blue bolts of a cold moon?
The voices of loneliness, the voices of sorrow
Lap at my back ineluctably.
How shall it soften them, this little lullaby?

How long can I be a wall around my green
        property?
How long can my hands
Be a bandage to his hurt, and my words
Bright birds in the sky, consoling, consoling?
It is a terrible thing
To be so open: it is as if my heart
Put on a face and walked into the world.

THIRD VOICE:
Today the colleges are drunk with spring.
My black gown is a little funeral:
It shows I am serious.
The books I carry wedge into my side.
I had an old wound once, but it is healing.
I had a dream of an island, red with cries.
It was a dream, and did not mean a thing.

Dawn flowers in the great elm outside the house.
The swifts are back. They are shrieking like paper
      rockets.
I hear the sound of the hours
Widen and die in the hedgerows. I hear the moo
      of cows.
The colors replenish themselves, and the wet
Thatch smokes in the sun.
The narcissi open white faces in the orchard.

I am reassured. I am reassured.
These are the clear bright colors of the nursery,
The talking ducks, the happy lambs.
I am simple again. I believe in miracles.
I do not believe in those terrible children
Who injure my sleep with their white eyes,
      their fingerless hands.
They are not mine. They do not belong to me.

I shall meditate upon normality.
I shall meditate upon my little son.
He does not walk. He does not speak a word.
He is still swaddled in white bands.
But he is pink and perfect. He smiles so frequently.
I have papered his room with big roses,
I have painted little hearts on everything.

I do not will him to be exceptional.
It is the exception that interests the devil.
It is the exception that climbs the sorrowful hill
Or sits in the desert and hurts his mother's heart.
I will him to be common,
To love me as I love him,
And to marry what he wants and where he will.

THIRD VOICE:
Hot noon in the meadows. The buttercups
Swelter and melt, and the lovers
Pass by, pass by.
They are black and flat as shadows.
It is so beautiful to have no attachments!
I am solitary as grass. What is it I miss?
Shall I ever find it, whatever it is?

The swans are gone. Still the river
Remembers how white they were.
It strives after them with its lights.
It finds their shapes in a cloud.
What is that bird that cries
With such sorrow in its voice?
I am young as ever, it says. What is it I miss?

SECOND VOICE:

I am at home in the lamplight. The evenings are
     lengthening.
I am mending a silk slip: my husband is reading.
How beautifully the light includes these things.
There is a kind of smoke in the spring air,
A smoke that takes the parks, the little statues
With pinkness, as if a tenderness awoke,
A tenderness that did not tire, something healing.

I wait and ache. I think I have been healing.
There is a great deal else to do. My hands
Can stitch lace neatly on to this material. My husband
Can turn and turn the pages of a book.
And so we are at home together, after hours.
It is only time that weighs upon our hands.
It is only time, and that is not material.

The streets may turn to paper suddenly, but I recover
From the long fall, and find myself in bed,
Safe on the mattress, hands braced, as for a fall.
I find myself again. I am no shadow
Though there is a shadow starting from my feet. I am
     a wife.
The city waits and aches. The little grasses
Crack through stone, and they are green with life.

142

LITTLE FUGUE

The yew's black fingers wag;
Cold clouds go over.
So the deaf and dumb
Signal the blind, and are ignored.

I like black statements.
The featurelessness of that cloud, now!
White as an eye all over!
The eye of the blind pianist

At my table on the ship.
He felt for his food.
His fingers had the noses of weasels.
I couldn't stop looking.

He could hear Beethoven:
Black yew, white cloud,
The horrific complications.
Finger-traps – a tumult of keys.

Empty and silly as plates,
So the blind smile.
I envy the big noises,
The yew hedge of the Grosse Fuge.

Deafness is something else.
Such a dark funnel, my father!
I see your voice
Black and leafy, as in my childhood,

A yew hedge of orders,
Gothic and barbarous, pure German.
Dead men cry from it.
I am guilty of nothing.

The yew my Christ, then.
Is it not as tortured?
And you, during the Great War
In the California delicatessen

Lopping the sausages!
They color my sleep,
Red, mottled, like cut necks.
There was a silence!

Great silence of another order.
I was seven, I knew nothing.
The world occurred.
You had one leg, and a Prussian mind.

Now similar clouds
Are spreading their vacuous sheets.

Do you say nothing?
I am lame in the memory.

I remember a blue eye,
A briefcase of tangerines.
This was a man, then!
Death opened, like a black tree, blackly.

I survive the while,
Arranging my morning.
These are my fingers, this my baby.
The clouds are a marriage dress, of that pallor.

AN APPEARANCE

The smile of iceboxes annihilates me.
Such blue currents in the veins of my loved one!
I hear her great heart purr.

From her lips ampersands and percent signs
Exit like kisses.
It is Monday in her mind: morals

Launder and present themselves.
What am I to make of these contradictions?
I wear white cuffs, I bow.

Is this love then, this red material
Issuing from the steel needle that flies so blindingly?
It will make little dresses and coats,

It will cover a dynasty.
How her body opens and shuts –
A Swiss watch, jeweled in the hinges!

O heart, such disorganization!
The stars are flashing like terrible numerals.
ABC, her eyelids say.

CROSSING THE WATER

Black lake, black boat, two black, cut-paper people.
Where do the black trees go that drink here?
Their shadows must cover Canada.

A little light is filtering from the water flowers.
Their leaves do not wish us to hurry:
They are round and flat and full of dark advice.

Cold worlds shake from the oar.
The spirit of blackness is in us, it is in the fishes.
A snag is lifting a valedictory, pale hand;

Stars open among the lilies.
Are you not blinded by such expressionless sirens?
This is the silence of astounded souls.

AMONG THE NARCISSI

Spry, wry, and gray as these March sticks,
Percy bows, in his blue peajacket, among the narcissi.
He is recuperating from something on the lung.

The narcissi, too, are bowing to some big thing:
It rattles their stars on the green hill where Percy
Nurses the hardship of his stitches, and walks
    and walks.

There is a dignity to this; there is a formality –
The flowers vivid as bandages, and the man mending.
They bow and stand: they suffer such attacks!

And the octogenarian loves the little flocks.
He is quite blue; the terrible wind tries his breathing.
The narcissi look up like children, quickly and whitely.

PHEASANT

You said you would kill it this morning.
Do not kill it. It startles me still,
The jut of that odd, dark head, pacing

Through the uncut grass on the elm's hill.
It is something to own a pheasant,
Or just to be visited at all.

I am not mystical: it isn't
As if I thought it had a spirit.
It is simply in its element.

That gives it a kingliness, a right.
The print of its big foot last winter,
The tail-track, on the snow in our court –

The wonder of it, in that pallor,
Through crosshatch of sparrow and starling.
Is it its rareness, then? It is rare.

But a dozen would be worth having,
A hundred, on that hill – green and red,
Crossing and recrossing: a fine thing!

It is such a good shape, so vivid.
It's a little cornucopia.
It unclaps, brown as a leaf, and loud,

Settles in the elm, and is easy.
It was sunning in the narcissi.
I trespass stupidly. Let be, let be.

ELM
For Ruth Fainlight

I know the bottom, she says. I know it with my great
    tap root:
It is what you fear.
I do not fear it: I have been there.

Is it the sea you hear in me,
Its dissatisfactions?
Or the voice of nothing, that was your madness?

Love is a shadow.
How you lie and cry after it
Listen: these are its hooves: it has gone off, like a horse.

All night I shall gallop thus, impetuously,
Till your head is a stone, your pillow a little turf,
Echoing, echoing.

Or shall I bring you the sound of poisons?
This is rain now, this big hush.
And this is the fruit of it: tin-white, like arsenic.

I have suffered the atrocity of sunsets.
Scorched to the root
My red filaments burn and stand, a hand of wires.

Now I break up in pieces that fly about like clubs.
A wind of such violence
Will tolerate no bystanding: I must shriek.

The moon, also, is merciless: she would drag me
Cruelly, being barren.
Her radiance scathes me. Or perhaps I have caught her.

I let her go. I let her go
Diminished and flat, as after radical surgery.
How your bad dreams possess and endow me.

I am inhabited by a cry.
Nightly it flaps out
Looking, with its hooks, for something to love.

I am terrified by this dark thing
That sleeps in me;
All day I feel its soft, feathery turnings, its malignity.

Clouds pass and disperse.
Are those the faces of love, those pale irretrievables?
Is it for such I agitate my heart?

I am incapable of more knowledge.
What is this, this face
So murderous in its strangle of branches?—

Its snaky acids hiss.
It petrifies the will. These are the isolate, slow faults
That kill, that kill, that kill.

THE RABBIT CATCHER

It was a place of force –
The wind gagging my mouth with my own blown hair,
Tearing off my voice, and the sea
Blinding me with its lights, the lives of the dead
Unreeling in it, spreading like oil.

I tasted the malignity of the gorse,
Its black spikes,
The extreme unction of its yellow candle-flowers.
They had an efficiency, a great beauty,
And were extravagant, like torture.

There was only one place to get to.
Simmering, perfumed,
The paths narrowed into the hollow.
And the snares almost effaced themselves –
Zeros, shutting on nothing,

Set close, like birth pangs.
The absence of shrieks
Made a hole in the hot day, a vacancy.
The glassy light was a clear wall,
The thickets quiet.

I felt a still busyness, an intent.
I felt hands round a tea mug, dull, blunt,
Ringing the white china.
How they awaited him, those little deaths!
They waited like sweethearts. They excited him.

And we, too, had a relationship –
Tight wires between us,
Pegs too deep to uproot, and a mind like a ring
Sliding shut on some quick thing,
The constriction killing me also.

EVENT

How the elements solidify! –
The moonlight, that chalk cliff
In whose rift we lie

Back to back. I hear an owl cry
From its cold indigo.
Intolerable vowels enter my heart.

The child in the white crib revolves and sighs,
Opens its mouth now, demanding.
His little face is carved in pained, red wood.

Then there are the stars – ineradicable, hard.
One touch: it burns and sickens.
I cannot see your eyes.

Where apple bloom ices the night
I walk in a ring,
A groove of old faults, deep and bitter.

Love cannot come here.
A black gap discloses itself.
On the opposite lip

A small white soul is waving, a small white maggot.
My limbs, also, have left me.
Who has dismembered us?

The dark is melting. We touch like cripples.

THE OTHER

You come in late, wiping your lips.
What did I leave untouched on the doorstep –

White Nike,
Streaming between my walls?

Smilingly, blue lightning
Assumes, like a meathook, the burden of his parts.

The police love you, you confess everything.
Bright hair, shoe-black, old plastic,

Is my life so intriguing?
Is it for this you widen your eye-rings?

Is it for this the air motes depart?
They are not air motes, they are corpuscles.

Open your handbag. What is that bad smell?
It is your knitting, busily

Hooking itself to itself,
It is your sticky candies.

I have your head on my wall.
Navel cords, blue-red and lucent,

Shriek from my belly like arrows, and these I ride.
O moon-glow, o sick one,

The stolen horses, the fornications
Circle a womb of marble.

Where are you going
That you suck breath like mileage?

Sulfurous adulteries grieve in a dream.
Cold glass, how you insert yourself

Between myself and myself.
I scratch like a cat.

The blood that runs is dark fruit –
An effect, a cosmetic.

You smile.
No, it is not fatal.

WORDS HEARD, BY ACCIDENT, OVER THE PHONE

O mud, mud, how fluid! –
Thick as foreign coffee, and with a sluggy pulse.
Speak, speak! Who is it?
It is the bowel-pulse, lover of digestibles.
It is he who has achieved these syllables.

What are these words, these words?
They are plopping like mud.
O god, how shall I ever clean the phone table?
They are pressing out of the many-holed earpiece,
        they are looking for a listener.
Is he here?

Now the room is ahiss. The instrument
Withdraws its tentacle.
But the spawn percolate in my heart. They are fertile.
Muck funnel, muck funnel –
You are too big. They must take you back!

POPPIES IN JULY

Little poppies, little hell flames,
Do you do no harm?

You flicker. I cannot touch you.
I put my hands among the flames. Nothing burns.

And it exhausts me to watch you
Flickering like that, wrinkly and clear red, like the skin
        of a mouth.

A mouth just bloodied.
Little bloody skirts!

There are fumes that I cannot touch.
Where are your opiates, your nauseous capsules?

If I could bleed, or sleep!—
If my mouth could marry a hurt like that!

Or your liquors seep to me, in this glass capsule,
Dulling and stilling.

But colorless. Colorless.

BURNING THE LETTERS

I made a fire; being tired
Of the white fists of old
Letters and their death rattle
When I came too close to the wastebasket.
What did they know that I didn't?
Grain by grain, they unrolled
Sands where a dream of clear water
Grinned like a getaway car.
I am not subtle
Love, love, and well, I was tired
Of cardboard cartons the color of cement or a dog pack
Holding in its hate
Dully, under a pack of men in red jackets,
And the eyes and times of the postmarks.

This fire may lick and fawn, but it is merciless:
A glass case
My fingers would enter although
They melt and sag, they are told
Do not touch.
And here is an end to the writing,
The spry hooks that bend and cringe, and the smiles,
        the smiles.
And at least it will be a good place now, the attic.
At least I won't be strung just under the surface,

Dumb fish
With one tin eye,
Watching for glints,
Riding my Arctic
Between this wish and that wish.

So I poke at the carbon birds in my housedress.
They are more beautiful than my bodiless owl,
They console me –
Rising and flying, but blinded.
They would flutter off, black and glittering, they
      would be coal angels
Only they have nothing to say to anybody.
I have seen to that.
With the butt of a rake
I flake up papers that breathe like people,
I fan them out
Between the yellow lettuces and the German cabbage
Involved in its weird blue dreams,
Involved as a foetus.
And a name with black edges

Wilts at my foot,
Sinuous orchis
In a nest of root-hairs and boredom –

Pale eyes, patent-leather gutturals!
Warm rain greases my hair, extinguishes nothing.
My veins glow like trees.
The dogs are tearing a fox. This is what it is like –
A red burst and a cry
That splits from its ripped bag and does not stop
With the dead eye
And the stuffed expression, but goes on
Dyeing the air,
Telling the particles of the clouds, the leaves, the water
What immortality is. That it is immortal.

FOR A FATHERLESS SON

You will be aware of an absence, presently,
Growing beside you, like a tree,
A death tree, color gone, an Australian gum tree –
Balding, gelded by lightning – an illusion,
And a sky like a pig's backside, an utter lack
    of attention.

But right now you are dumb.
And I love your stupidity,
The blind mirror of it. I look in
And find no face but my own, and you think
    that's funny.
It is good for me

To have you grab my nose, a ladder rung.
One day you may touch what's wrong
The small skulls, the smashed blue hills, the
    godawful hush.
Till then your smiles are found money.

A BIRTHDAY PRESENT

What is this, behind this veil, is it ugly, is it beautiful?
It is shimmering, has it breasts, has it edges?

I am sure it is unique, I am sure it is just what I want.
When I am quiet at my cooking I feel it looking,
    I feel it thinking

'Is this the one I am to appear for,
Is this the elect one, the one with black eye-pits
    and a scar?

Measuring the flour, cutting off the surplus,
Adhering to rules, to rules, to rules.

Is this the one for the annunciation?
My god, what a laugh!'

But it shimmers, it does not stop, and I think it wants me.
I would not mind if it was bones, or a pearl button.

I do not want much of a present, anyway, this year.
After all I am alive only by accident.

I would have killed myself gladly that time any
    possible way.
Now there are these veils, shimmering like curtains,

The diaphanous satins of a January window
White as babies' bedding and glittering with dead
        breath. O ivory!

It must be a tusk there, a ghost-column.
Can you not see I do not mind what it is.

Can you not give it to me?
Do not be ashamed – I do not mind if it is small.

Do not be mean, I am ready for enormity.
Let us sit down to it, one on either side, admiring
        the gleam,

The glaze, the mirrory variety of it.
Let us eat our last supper at it, like a hospital plate.

I know why you will not give it to me,
You are terrified

The world will go up in a shriek, and your head with it,
Bossed, brazen, an antique shield,

A marvel to your great-grandchildren.
Do not be afraid, it is not so.

I will only take it and go aside quietly.
You will not even hear me opening it, no paper crackle,

No falling ribbons, no scream at the end.
I do not think you credit me with this discretion.

If you only knew how the veils were killing my days.
To you they are only transparencies, clear air.

But my god, the clouds are like cotton.
Armies of them. They are carbon monoxide.

Sweetly, sweetly I breathe in,
Filling my veins with invisibles, with the million

Probable motes that tick the years off my life.
You are silver-suited for the occasion. O adding
        machine—

Is it impossible for you to let something go and have
        it go whole?
Must you stamp each piece in purple,

Must you kill what you can?
There is this one thing I want today, and only you can
        give it to me.

It stands at my window, big as the sky.
It breathes from my sheets, the cold dead center

Where spilt lives congeal and stiffen to history.
Let it not come by the mail, finger by finger.

Let it not come by word of mouth, I should be sixty
By the time the whole of it was delivered, and too
    numb to use it.

Only let down the veil, the veil, the veil.
If it were death

I would admire the deep gravity of it, its timeless eyes.
I would know you were serious.

There would be a nobility then, there would be a
    birthday.
And the knife not carve, but enter

Pure and clean as the cry of a baby,
And the universe slide from my side.

THE DETECTIVE

What was she doing when it blew in
Over the seven hills, the red furrow, the blue
    mountain?
Was she arranging cups? It is important.
Was she at the window, listening?
In that valley the train shrieks echo like souls on hooks.

That is the valley of death, though the cows thrive.
In her garden the lies were shaking out their
    moist silks
And the eyes of the killer moving sluglike and sidelong,
Unable to face the fingers, those egotists.
The fingers were tamping a woman into a wall,

A body into a pipe, and the smoke rising.
This is the smell of years burning, here in the kitchen,
These are the deceits, tacked up like family
    photographs,
And this is a man, look at his smile,
The death weapon? No one is dead.

There is no body in the house at all.
There is the smell of polish, there are plush carpets.
There is the sunlight, playing its blades,
Bored hoodlum in a red room

Where the wireless talks to itself like an elderly
    relative.

Did it come like an arrow, did it come like a knife?
Which of the poisons is it?
Which of the nerve-curlers, the convulsors?
    Did it electrify?
This is a case without a body.
The body does not come into it at all.

It is a case of vaporization.
The mouth first, its absence reported
In the second year. It had been insatiable
And in punishment was hung out like brown fruit
To wrinkle and dry.

The breasts next.
These were harder, two white stones.
The milk came yellow, then blue and sweet as water.
There was no absence of lips, there were two children,
But their bones showed, and the moon smiled.

Then the dry wood, the gates,
The brown motherly furrows, the whole estate.
We walk on air, Watson.
There is only the moon, embalmed in phosphorus.
There is only a crow in a tree. Make notes.

THE COURAGE OF SHUTTING-UP

The courage of the shut mouth, in spite of artillery!
The line pink and quiet, a worm, basking.
There are black disks behind it, the disks of outrage,
And the outrage of a sky, the lined brain of it.
The disks revolve, they ask to be heard –

Loaded, as they are, with accounts of bastardies.
Bastardies, usages, desertions and doubleness,
The needle journeying in its groove,
Silver beast between two dark canyons,
A great surgeon, now a tattooist,

Tattooing over and over the same blue grievances,
The snakes, the babies, the tits
On mermaids and two-legged dreamgirls.
The surgeon is quiet, he does not speak.
He has seen too much death, his hands are full of it.

So the disks of the brain revolve, like the muzzles
        of cannon.
Then there is that antique billhook, the tongue,
Indefatigable, purple. Must it be cut out?
It has nine tails, it is dangerous.
And the noise it flays from the air, once it gets going!

No, the tongue, too, has been put by,
Hung up in the library with the engravings
    of Rangoon
And the fox heads, the otter heads, the heads
    of dead rabbits.
It is a marvelous object –
The things it has pierced in its time.

But how about the eyes, the eyes, the eyes?
Mirrors can kill and talk, they are terrible rooms
In which a torture goes on one can only watch.
The face that lived in this mirror is the face of a
    dead man.
Do not worry about the eyes –

They may be white and shy, they are no stool pigeons,
Their death rays folded like flags
Of a country no longer heard of,
An obstinate independency
Insolvent among the mountains.

THE BEE MEETING

Who are these people at the bridge to meet me? They
      are the villagers—
The rector, the midwife, the sexton, the agent for bees.
In my sleeveless summery dress I have no protection,
And they are all gloved and covered, why did nobody
      tell me?
They are smiling and taking out veils tacked to
      ancient hats.

I am nude as a chicken neck, does nobody love me?
Yes, here is the secretary of bees with her white
      shop smock,
Buttoning the cuffs at my wrists and the slit from my
      neck to my knees.
Now I am milkweed silk, the bees will not notice.
They will not smell my fear, my fear, my fear.

Which is the rector now, is it that man in black?
Which is the midwife, is that her blue coat?
Everybody is nodding a square black head, they are
      knights in visors,
Breastplates of cheesecloth knotted under the armpits.
Their smiles and their voices are changing. I am led
      through a beanfield.

Strips of tinfoil winking like people,
Feather dusters fanning their hands in a sea of
	bean flowers,
Creamy bean flowers with black eyes and leaves like
	bored hearts.
Is it blood clots the tendrils are dragging up that string?
No, no, it is scarlet flowers that will one day be edible.

Now they are giving me a fashionable white straw
	Italian hat
And a black veil that molds to my face, they are making
	me one of them.
They are leading me to the shorn grove, the circle
	of hives.
Is it the hawthorn that smells so sick?
The barren body of hawthorn, etherizing its children.

Is it some operation that is taking place?
It is the surgeon my neighbors are waiting for,
This apparition in a green helmet,
Shining gloves and white suit.
Is it the butcher, the grocer, the postman, someone
	I know?

I cannot run, I am rooted, and the gorse hurts me
With its yellow purses, its spiky armory.
I could not run without having to run forever.
The white hive is snug as a virgin,
Sealing off her brood cells, her honey, and quietly
      humming.

Smoke rolls and scarves in the grove.
The mind of the hive thinks this is the end of every
Here they come, the outriders, on their hysterical
      elastics.
If I stand very still, they will think I am cow-parsl
A gullible head untouched by their animosity,

Not even nodding, a personage in a hedgerow.
The villagers open the chambers, they are hunting
      the queen.
Is she hiding, is she eating honey? She is very clev
She is old, old, old, she must live another year,
      and she knows it.
While in their fingerjoint cells the new virgins

Dream of a duel they will win inevitably,
A curtain of wax dividing them from the bride flig
The upflight of the murderess into a heaven that
      loves her.

The villagers are moving the virgins, there will be
     no killing.
The old queen does not show herself, is she so
     ungrateful?

I am exhausted, I am exhausted—
Pillar of white in a blackout of knives.
I am the magician's girl who does not flinch.
The villagers are untying their disguises, they are
     shaking hands.
Whose is that long white box in the grove, what have
     they accomplished, why am I cold.

THE ARRIVAL OF THE BEE BOX

I ordered this, this clean wood box
Square as a chair and almost too heavy to lift.
I would say it was the coffin of a midget
Or a square baby
Were there not such a din in it.

The box is locked, it is dangerous.
I have to live with it overnight
And I can't keep away from it.
There are no windows, so I can't see what is in there.
There is only a little grid, no exit.

I put my eye to the grid.
It is dark, dark,
With the swarmy feeling of African hands
Minute and shrunk for export,
Black on black, angrily clambering.

How can I let them out?
It is the noise that appalls me most of all,
The unintelligible syllables.
It is like a Roman mob,
Small, taken one by one, but my god, together!

I lay my ear to furious Latin.
I am not a Caesar.
I have simply ordered a box of maniacs.
They can be sent back.
They can die, I need feed them nothing,
    I am the owner.

I wonder how hungry they are.
I wonder if they would forget me
If I just undid the locks and stood back and turned
    into a tree.
There is the laburnum, its blond colonnades,
And the petticoats of the cherry.

They might ignore me immediately
In my moon suit and funeral veil.
I am no source of honey
So why should they turn on me?
Tomorrow I will be sweet God, I will set them free.

The box is only temporary.

STINGS

Bare-handed, I hand the combs.
The man in white smiles, bare-handed,
Our cheesecloth gauntlets neat and sweet,
The throats of our wrists brave lilies.
He and I

Have a thousand clean cells between us,
Eight combs of yellow cups,
And the hive itself a teacup,
White with pink flowers on it,
With excessive love I enameled it

Thinking 'Sweetness, sweetness'.
Brood cells gray as the fossils of shells
Terrify me, they seem so old.
What am I buying, wormy mahogany?
Is there any queen at all in it?

If there is, she is old,
Her wings torn shawls, her long body
Rubbed of its plush—
Poor and bare and unqueenly and even shameful.
I stand in a column

Of winged, unmiraculous women,
Honey-drudgers.

I am no drudge
Though for years I have eaten dust
And dried plates with my dense hair.

And seen my strangeness evaporate,
Blue dew from dangerous skin.
Will they hate me,
These women who only scurry,
Whose news is the open cherry, the open clover?

It is almost over.
I am in control.
Here is my honey-machine,
It will work without thinking,
Opening, in spring, like an industrious virgin

To scour the creaming crests
As the moon, for its ivory powders, scours the sea.
A third person is watching.
He has nothing to do with the bee-seller or with me.
Now he is gone

In eight great bounds, a great scapegoat.
Here is his slipper, here is another,
And here the square of white linen
He wore instead of a hat.

He was sweet,

The sweat of his efforts a rain
Tugging the world to fruit.
The bees found him out,
Molding onto his lips like lies,
Complicating his features.

They thought death was worth it, but I
Have a self to recover, a queen.
Is she dead, is she sleeping?
Where has she been,
With her lion-red body, her wings of glass?

Now she is flying
More terrible than she ever was, red
Scar in the sky, red comet
Over the engine that killed her—
The mausoleum, the wax house.

THE SWARM

Somebody is shooting at something in our town –
A dull pom, pom in the Sunday street.
Jealousy can open the blood,
It can make black roses.
Who are they shooting at?

It is you the knives are out for
At Waterloo, Waterloo, Napoleon,
The hump of Elba on your short back,
And the snow, marshaling its brilliant cutlery
Mass after mass, saying Shh!

Shh! These are chess people you play with,
Still figures of ivory.
The mud squirms with throats,
Stepping stones for French bootsoles.
The gilt and pink domes of Russia melt and float off

In the furnace of greed. Clouds, clouds.
So the swarm balls and deserts
Seventy feet up, in a black pine tree.
It must be shot down. Pom! Pom!
So dumb it thinks bullets are thunder.

It thinks they are the voice of God
Condoning the beak, the claw, the grin of the dog
Yellow-haunched, a pack-dog,
Grinning over its bone of ivory
Like the pack, the pack, like everybody.

The bees have got so far. Seventy feet high!
Russia, Poland and Germany!
The mild hills, the same old magenta
Fields shrunk to a penny
Spun into a river, the river crossed.

The bees argue, in their black ball,
A flying hedgehog, all prickles.
The man with gray hands stands under the honeycomb
Of their dream, the hived station
Where trains, faithful to their steel arcs,

Leave and arrive, and there is no end to the country.
Pom! Pom! They fall
Dismembered, to a tod of ivy.
So much for the charioteers, the outriders, the Grand
        Army!
A red tatter, Napoleon!

The last badge of victory.
The swarm is knocked into a cocked straw hat.

Elba, Elba, bleb on the sea!
The white busts of marshals, admirals, generals
Worming themselves into niches.

How instructive this is!
The dumb, banded bodies
Walking the plank draped with Mother France's
     upholstery
Into a new mausoleum,
An ivory palace, a crotch pine.

The man with gray hands smiles –
The smile of a man of business, intensely practical.
They are not hands at all
But asbestos receptacles.
Pom! Pom! 'They would have killed *me*.'

Stings big as drawing pins!
It seems bees have a notion of honor,
A black intractable mind.
Napoleon is pleased, he is pleased with everything.
O Europe! O ton of honey!

WINTERING

This is the easy time, there is nothing doing.
I have whirled the midwife's extractor,
I have my honey,
Six jars of it,
Six cat's eyes in the wine cellar,

Wintering in a dark without window
At the heart of the house
Next to the last tenant's rancid jam
And the bottles of empty glitters—
Sir So-and-so's gin.

This is the room I have never been in.
This is the room I could never breathe in.
The black bunched in there like a bat,
No light
But the torch and its faint

Chinese yellow on appalling objects—
Black asininity. Decay.
Possession.
It is they who own me.
Neither cruel nor indifferent,

Only ignorant.
This is the time of hanging on for the bees – the bees
So slow I hardly know them,
Filing like soldiers
To the syrup tin

To make up for the honey I've taken.
Tate and Lyle keeps them going,
The refined snow.
It is Tate and Lyle they live on, instead of flowers.
They take it. The cold sets in.

Now they ball in a mass,
Black
Mind against all that white.
The smile of the snow is white.
It spreads itself out, a mile-long body of Meissen,

Into which, on warm days,
They can only carry their dead.
The bees are all women,
Maids and the long royal lady.
They have got rid of the men,

The blunt, clumsy stumblers, the boors.
Winter is for women—
The woman, still at her knitting,
At the cradle of Spanish walnut,
Her body a bulb in the cold and too dumb to think.

Will the hive survive, will the gladiolas
Succeed in banking their fires
To enter another year?
What will they taste of, the Christmas roses?
The bees are flying. They taste the spring.

THE APPLICANT

First, are you our sort of a person?
Do you wear
A glass eye, false teeth or a crutch,
A brace or a hook,
Rubber breasts or a rubber crotch,

Stitches to show something's missing?
    No, no? Then
How can we give you a thing?
Stop crying.
Open your hand.
Empty? Empty. Here is a hand

To fill it and willing
To bring teacups and roll away headaches
And do whatever you tell it.
Will you marry it?
It is guaranteed

To thumb shut your eyes at the end
And dissolve of sorrow.
We make new stock from the salt.
I notice you are stark naked.
How about this suit—

Black and stiff, but not a bad fit.
Will you marry it?
It is waterproof, shatterproof, proof
Against fire and bombs through the roof.
Believe me, they'll bury you in it.

Now your head, excuse me, is empty.
I have the ticket for that.
Come here, sweetie, out of the closet.
Well, what do you think of *that*?
Naked as paper to start

But in twenty-five years she'll be silver,
In fifty, gold.
A living doll, everywhere you look.
It can sew, it can cook,
It can talk, talk, talk.

It works, there is nothing wrong with it.
You have a hole, it's a poultice.
You have an eye, it's an image.
My boy, it's your last resort.
Will you marry it, marry it, marry it.

DADDY

You do not do, you do not do
Any more, black shoe
In which I have lived like a foot
For thirty years, poor and white,
Barely daring to breathe or Achoo.

Daddy, I have had to kill you.
You died before I had time—
Marble-heavy, a bag full of God,
Ghastly statue with one gray toe
Big as a Frisco seal

And a head in the freakish Atlantic
Where it pours bean green over blue
In the waters off beautiful Nauset.
I used to pray to recover you.
Ach, du.

In the German tongue, in the Polish town
Scraped flat by the roller
Of wars, wars, wars.
But the name of the town is common.
My Polack friend

Says there are a dozen or two.
So I never could tell where you
Put your foot, your root,
I never could talk to you.
The tongue stuck in my jaw.

It stuck in a barb wire snare.
Ich, ich, ich, ich,
I could hardly speak.
I thought every German was you.
And the language obscene

An engine, an engine
Chuffing me off like a Jew.
A Jew to Dachau, Auschwitz, Belsen.
I began to talk like a Jew.
I think I may well be a Jew.

The snows of the Tyrol, the clear beer of Vienna
Are not very pure or true.
With my gipsy ancestress and my weird luck
And my Taroc pack and my Taroc pack
I may be a bit of a Jew.

I have always been scared of *you*,
With your Luftwaffe, your gobbledygoo.
And your neat mustache

And your Aryan eye, bright blue.
Panzer-man, panzer-man, O You—

Not God but a swastika
So black no sky could squeak through.
Every woman adores a Fascist,
The boot in the face, the brute
Brute heart of a brute like you.

You stand at the blackboard, daddy,
In the picture I have of you,
A cleft in your chin instead of your foot
But no less a devil for that, no not
Any less the black man who

Bit my pretty red heart in two.
I was ten when they buried you.
At twenty I tried to die
And get back, back, back to you.
I thought even the bones would do.

But they pulled me out of the sack,
And they stuck me together with glue.
And then I knew what to do.
I made a model of you,
A man in black with a Meinkampf look

And a love of the rack and the screw.
And I said I do, I do.
So daddy, I'm finally through.
The black telephone's off at the root,
The voices just can't worm through.

If I've killed one man, I've killed two—
The vampire who said he was you
And drank my blood for a year,
Seven years, if you want to know.
Daddy, you can lie back now.

There's a stake in your fat black heart
And the villagers never liked you.
They are dancing and stamping on you.
They always *knew* it was you.
Daddy, daddy, you bastard, I'm through.

MEDUSA

Off that landspit of stony mouth-plugs,
Eyes rolled by white sticks,
Ears cupping the sea's incoherences,
You house your unnerving head – God-ball,
Lens of mercies,

Your stooges
Plying their wild cells in my keel's shadow,
Pushing by like hearts,
Red stigmata at the very center,
Riding the rip tide to the nearest point of departure,

Dragging their Jesus hair.
Did I escape, I wonder?
My mind winds to you
Old barnacled umbilicus, Atlantic cable,
Keeping itself, it seems, in a state of miraculous repair.

In any case, you are always there,
Tremulous breath at the end of my line,
Curve of water upleaping
To my water rod, dazzling and grateful,
Touching and sucking.

I didn't call you.
I didn't call you at all.
Nevertheless, nevertheless
You steamed to me over the sea,
Fat and red, a placenta

Paralysing the kicking lovers.
Cobra light
Squeezing the breath from the blood bells
Of the fuchsia. I could draw no breath,
Dead and moneyless,

Overexposed, like an X-ray.
Who do you think you are?
A Communion wafer? Blubbery Mary?
I shall take no bite of your body,
Bottle in which I live,

Ghastly Vatican.
I am sick to death of hot salt.
Green as eunuchs, your wishes
Hiss at my sins.
Off, off, eely tentacle!

There is nothing between us.

FEVER 103°

Pure? What does it mean?
The tongues of hell
Are dull, dull as the triple

Tongues of dull, fat Cerberus
Who wheezes at the gate. Incapable
Of licking clean

The aguey tendon, the sin, the sin.
The tinder cries.
The indelible smell

Of a snuffed candle!
Love, love, the low smokes roll
From me like Isadora's scarves, I'm in a fright

One scarf will catch and anchor in the wheel.
Such yellow sullen smokes
Make their own element. They will not rise,

But trundle round the globe
Choking the aged and the meek,
The weak

Hothouse baby in its crib,
The ghastly orchid
Hanging its hanging garden in the air,

Devilish leopard!
Radiation turned it white
And killed it in an hour.

Greasing the bodies of adulterers
Like Hiroshima ash and eating in.
The sin. The sin.

Darling, all night
I have been flickering, off, on, off, on.
The sheets grow heavy as a lecher's kiss.

Three days. Three nights.
Lemon water, chicken
Water, water make me retch.

I am too pure for you or anyone.
Your body
Hurts me as the world hurts God. I am a lantern-

My head a moon
Of Japanese paper, my gold beaten skin
Infinitely delicate and infinitely expensive.

Does not my heat astound you. And my light.
All by myself I am a huge camellia
Glowing and coming and going, flush on flush.

I think I am going up,
I think I may rise—
The beads of hot metal fly, and I, love, I

Am a pure acetylene
Virgin
Attended by roses,

By kisses, by cherubim,
By whatever these pink things mean.
Not you, nor him

Not him, nor him
(My selves dissolving, old whore petticoats)—
To Paradise.

AMNESIAC

No use, no use, now, begging Recognize!
There is nothing to do with such a beautiful blank but
    smooth it.
Name, house, car keys,

The little toy wife –
Erased, sigh, sigh.
Four babies and a cocker!

Nurses the size of worms and a minute doctor
Tuck him in.
Old happenings

Peel from his skin.
Down the drain with all of it!
Hugging his pillow

Like the red-headed sister he never dared to touch,
He dreams of a new one –
Barren, the lot are barren!

And of another color.
How they'll travel, travel, travel, scenery
Sparking off their brother-sister rears

A comet tail!
And money the sperm fluid of it all.
One nurse brings in

A green drink, one a blue.
They rise on either side of him like stars.
The two drinks flame and foam.

O sister, mother, wife,
Sweet Lethe is my life.
I am never, never, never coming home!

CUT
For Susan O'Neill Roe

What a thrill—
My thumb instead of an onion.
The top quite gone
Except for a sort of a hinge

Of skin,
A flap like a hat,
Dead white.
Then that red plush.

Little pilgrim,
The Indian's axed your scalp.
Your turkey wattle
Carpet rolls

Straight from the heart.
I step on it,
Clutching my bottle
Of pink fizz.

A celebration, this is.
Out of a gap
A million soldiers run,
Redcoats, every one.

Whose side are they on?
O my
Homunculus, I am ill.
I have taken a pill to kill

The thin
Papery feeling.
Saboteur,
Kamikaze man—

The stain on your
Gauze Ku Klux Klan
Babushka
Darkens and tarnishes and when

The balled
Pulp of your heart
Confronts its small
Mill of silence

How you jump—
Trepanned veteran,
Dirty girl,
Thumb stump.

BY CANDLELIGHT

This is winter, this is night, small love –
A sort of black horsehair,
A rough, dumb country stuff
Steeled with the sheen
Of what green stars can make it to our gate.
I hold you on my arm.
It is very late.
The dull bells tongue the hour.
The mirror floats us at one candle power.

This is the fluid in which we meet each other,
This haloey radiance that seems to breathe
And lets our shadows wither
Only to blow
Them huge again, violent giants on the wall.
One match scratch makes you real.
At first the candle will not bloom at all –
It snuffs its bud
To almost nothing, to a dull blue dud.

I hold my breath until you creak to life,
Balled hedgehog,
Small and cross. The yellow knife
Grows tall. You clutch your bars.
My singing makes you roar.

I rock you like a boat
Across the Indian carpet, the cold floor,
While the brass man
Kneels, back bent, as best he can

Hefting his white pillar with the light
That keeps the sky at bay,
The sack of black! It is everywhere, tight, tight!
He is yours, the little brassy Atlas –
Poor heirloom, all you have,
At his heels a pile of five brass cannonballs,
No child, no wife.
Five balls! Five bright brass balls!
To juggle with, my love, when the sky falls.

ARIEL

Stasis in darkness.
Then the substanceless blue
Pour of tor and distances.

God's lioness,
How one we grow,
Pivot of heels and knees! – The furrow

Splits and passes, sister to
The brown arc
Of the neck I cannot catch,

Nigger-eye
Berries cast dark
Hooks—

Black sweet blood mouthfuls,
Shadows.
Something else

Hauls me through air—
Thighs, hair;
Flakes from my heels.

White
Godiva, I unpeel—
Dead hands, dead stringencies.

And now I
Foam to wheat, a glitter of seas.
The child's cry

Melts in the wall.
And I
Am the arrow,

The dew that flies
Suicidal, at one with the drive
Into the red

Eye, the cauldron of morning.

POPPIES IN OCTOBER

Even the sun-clouds this morning cannot manage
        such skirts.
Nor the woman in the ambulance
Whose red heart blooms through her coat so
        astoundingly—

A gift, a love gift
Utterly unasked for
By a sky

Palely and flamily
Igniting its carbon monoxides, by eyes
Dulled to a halt under bowlers.

O my God, what am I
That these late mouths should cry open
In a forest of frost, in a dawn of cornflowers.

NICK AND THE CANDLESTICK

I am a miner. The light burns blue.
Waxy stalacmites
Drip and thicken, tears

The earthen womb
Exudes from its dead boredom.
Black bat airs

Wrap me, raggy shawls,
Cold homicides.
They weld to me like plums.

Old cave of calcium
Icicles, old echoer.
Even the newts are white,

Those holy Joes.
And the fish, the fish—
Christ! they are panes of ice,

A vice of knives,
A piranha
Religion, drinking

Its first communion out of my live toes.
The candle
Gulps and recovers its small altitude,

Its yellows hearten.
O love, how did you get here?
O embryo

Remembering, even in sleep,
Your crossed position.
The blood blooms clean

In you, ruby.
The pain
You wake to is not yours.

Love, love,
I have hung our cave with roses,
With soft rugs—

The last of Victoriana.
Let the stars
Plummet to their dark address,

Let the mercuric
Atoms that cripple drip
Into the terrible well,

You are the one
Solid the spaces lean on, envious.
You are the baby in the barn.

LADY LAZARUS

I have done it again.
One year in every ten
I manage it—

A sort of walking miracle, my skin
Bright as a Nazi lampshade,
My right foot

A paperweight,
My face a featureless, fine
Jew linen.

Peel off the napkin
O my enemy.
Do I terrify?—

The nose, the eye pits, the full set of teeth?
The sour breath
Will vanish in a day.

Soon, soon the flesh
The grave cave ate will be
At home on me

And I a smiling woman.
I am only thirty.
And like the cat I have nine times to die.

This is Number Three.
What a trash
To annihilate each decade.

What a million filaments.
The peanut-crunching crowd
Shoves in to see

Them unwrap me hand and foot—
The big strip tease.
Gentlemen, ladies

These are my hands
My knees.
I may be skin and bone,

Nevertheless, I am the same, identical woman.
The first time it happened I was ten.
It was an accident.

The second time I meant
To last it out and not come back at all.
I rocked shut

As a seashell.
They had to call and call
And pick the worms off me like sticky pearls.

Dying
Is an art, like everything else.
I do it exceptionally well.

I do it so it feels like hell.
I do it so it feels real.
I guess you could say I've a call.

It's easy enough to do it in a cell.
It's easy enough to do it and stay put.
It's the theatrical

Comeback in broad day
To the same place, the same face, the same brute
Amused shout:

'A miracle!'
That knocks me out.
There is a charge

For the eyeing of my scars, there is a charge
For the hearing of my heart—
It really goes.

And there is a charge, a very large charge
For a word or a touch
Or a bit of blood

Or a piece of my hair or my clothes.
So, so, Herr Doktor.
So, Herr Enemy.

I am your opus,
I am your valuable,
The pure gold baby

That melts to a shriek.
I turn and burn.
Do not think I underestimate your great concern.

Ash, ash –
You poke and stir.
Flesh, bone, there is nothing there—

A cake of soap,
A wedding ring,
A gold filling.

Herr God, Herr Lucifer
Beware
Beware.

Out of the ash
I rise with my red hair
And I eat men like air.

DEATH & CO.

Two, of course there are two.
It seems perfectly natural now—
The one who never looks up, whose eyes are lidded
And balled, like Blake's,
Who exhibits

The birthmarks that are his trademark—
The scald scar of water,
The nude
Verdigris of the condor.
I am red meat. His beak

Claps sidewise: I am not his yet.
He tells me how badly I photograph.
He tells me how sweet
The babies look in their hospital
Icebox, a simple

Frill at the neck,
Then the flutings of their Ionian
Death-gowns,
Then two little feet.
He does not smile or smoke.

The other does that,
His hair long and plausive.
Bastard
Masturbating a glitter,
He wants to be loved.

I do not stir.
The frost makes a flower,
The dew makes a star,
The dead bell,
The dead bell.

Somebody's done for.

WINTER TREES

The wet dawn inks are doing their blue dissolve.
On their blotter of fog the trees
Seem a botanical drawing –
Memories growing, ring on ring,
A series of weddings.

Knowing neither abortions nor bitchery,
Truer than women,
They seed so effortlessly!
Tasting the winds, that are footless,
Waist-deep in history –

Full of wings, otherworldliness.
In this, they are Ledas.
O mother of leaves and sweetness
Who are these pietàs?
The shadows of ringdoves chanting, but easing
        nothing.

CHILDLESS WOMAN

The womb
Rattles its pod, the moon
Discharges itself from the tree with nowhere to go.

My landscape is a hand with no lines,
The roads bunched to a knot,
The knot myself,

Myself the rose you achieve –
This body,
This ivory

Ungodly as a child's shriek.
Spiderlike, I spin mirrors,
Loyal to my image,

Uttering nothing but blood –
Taste it, dark red!
And my forest

My funeral,
And this hill and this
Gleaming with the mouths of corpses.

1963

SHEEP IN FOG

The hills step off into whiteness.
People or stars
Regard me sadly, I disappoint them.

The train leaves a line of breath.
O slow
Horse the color of rust,

Hooves, dolorous bells—
All morning the
Morning has been blackening,

A flower left out.
My bones hold a stillness, the far
Fields melt my heart.

They threaten
To let me through to a heaven
Starless and fatherless, a dark water.

THE MUNICH MANNEQUINS

Perfection is terrible, it cannot have children.
Cold as snow breath, it tamps the womb

Where the yew trees blow like hydras,
The tree of life and the tree of life

Unloosing their moons, month after month,
    to no purpose.
The blood flood is the flood of love,

The absolute sacrifice.
It means: no more idols but me,

Me and you.
So, in their sulfur loveliness, in their smiles

These mannequins lean tonight
In Munich, morgue between Paris and Rome,

Naked and bald in their furs,
Orange lollies on silver sticks,

Intolerable, without mind.
The snow drops its pieces of darkness,

Nobody's about. In the hotels
Hands will be opening doors and setting

Down shoes for a polish of carbon
Into which broad toes will go tomorrow.

O the domesticity of these windows,
The baby lace, the green-leaved confectionery,

The thick Germans slumbering in their bottomless
        Stolz.
And the black phones on hooks

Glittering
Glittering and digesting

Voicelessness. The snow has no voice.

TOTEM

The engine is killing the track, the track is silver,
It stretches into the distance. It will be eaten
    nevertheless.

Its running is useless.
At nightfall there is the beauty of drowned fields,

Dawn gilds the farmers like pigs,
Swaying slightly in their thick suits,

White towers of Smithfield ahead,
Fat haunches and blood on their minds.

There is no mercy in the glitter of cleavers,
The butcher's guillotine that whispers: 'How's this,
    how's this?'

In the bowl the hare is aborted,
Its baby head out of the way, embalmed in spice,

Flayed of fur and humanity.
Let us eat it like Plato's afterbirth,

Let us eat it like Christ.
These are the people that were important—

Their round eyes, their teeth, their grimaces
On a stick that rattles and clicks, a counterfeit snake.

Shall the hood of the cobra appall me—
The loneliness of its eye, the eye of the mountains

Through which the sky eternally threads itself?
The world is blood-hot and personal

Dawn says, with its blood-flush.
There is no terminus, only suitcases

Out of which the same self unfolds like a suit
Bald and shiny, with pockets of wishes,

Notions and tickets, short circuits and folding mirrors.
I am mad, calls the spider, waving its many arms.

And in truth it is terrible,
Multiplied in the eyes of the flies.

They buzz like blue children
In nets of the infinite,

Roped in at the end by the one
Death with its many sticks.

CHILD

Your clear eye is the one absolutely beautiful thing.
I want to fill it with color and ducks,
The zoo of the new

Whose names you meditate –
April snowdrop, Indian pipe,
Little

Stalk without wrinkle,
Pool in which images
Should be grand and classical

Not this troublous
Wringing of hands, this dark
Ceiling without a star.

PARALYTIC

It happens. Will it go on?—
My mind a rock,
No fingers to grip, no tongue,
My god the iron lung

That loves me, pumps
My two
Dust bags in and out,
Will not

Let me relapse
While the day outside glides by like ticker tape.
The night brings violets,
Tapestries of eyes,

Lights,
The soft anonymous
Talkers: 'You all right?'
The starched, inaccessible breast.

Dead egg, I lie
Whole
On a whole world I cannot touch,
At the white, tight

Drum of my sleeping couch
Photographs visit me—
My wife, dead and flat, in 1920 furs,
Mouth full of pearls,

Two girls
As flat as she, who whisper 'We're your daughters.'
The still waters
Wrap my lips,

Eyes, nose and ears,
A clear
Cellophane I cannot crack.
On my bare back

I smile, a buddha, all
Wants, desire
Falling from me like rings
Hugging their lights.

The claw
Of the magnolia,
Drunk on its own scents,
Asks nothing of life.

GIGOLO

Pocket watch, I tick well.
The streets are lizardy crevices
Sheer-sided, with holes where to hide.
It is best to meet in a cul-de-sac,

A palace of velvet
With windows of mirrors.
There one is safe,
There are no family photographs,

No rings through the nose, no cries.
Bright fish hooks, the smiles of women
Gulp at my bulk
And I, in my snazzy blacks,

Mill a litter of breasts like jellyfish.
To nourish
The cellos of moans I eat eggs –
Eggs and fish, the essentials,

The aphrodisiac squid.
My mouth sags,
The mouth of Christ
When my engine reaches the end of it.

The tattle of my
Gold joints, my way of turning
Bitches to ripples of silver
Rolls out a carpet, a hush.

And there is no end, no end of it.
I shall never grow old. New oysters
Shriek in the sea and I
Glitter like Fontainebleau

Gratified,
All the fall of water an eye
Over whose pool I tenderly
Lean and see me.

MYSTIC

The air is a mill of hooks –
Questions without answer,
Glittering and drunk as flies
Whose kiss stings unbearably
In the fetid wombs of black air under pines in summer.

I remember
The dead smell of sun on wood cabins,
The stiffness of sails, the long salt winding sheets.
Once one has seen God, what is the remedy?
Once one has been seized up

Without a part left over,
Not a toe, not a finger, and used,
Used utterly, in the sun's conflagrations, the stains
That lengthen from ancient cathedrals
What is the remedy?

The pill of the Communion tablet,
The walking beside still water? Memory?
Or picking up the bright pieces
Of Christ in the faces of rodents,
The tame flower-nibblers, the ones

Whose hopes are so low they are comfortable –
The humpback in his small, washed cottage
Under the spokes of the clematis.
Is there no great love, only tenderness?
Does the sea

Remember the walker upon it?
Meaning leaks from the molecules.
The chimneys of the city breathe, the window sweats,
The children leap in their cots.
The sun blooms, it is a geranium.

The heart has not stopped.

KINDNESS

Kindness glides about my house.
Dame Kindness, she is so nice!
The blue and red jewels of her rings smoke
In the windows, the mirrors
Are filling with smiles.

What is so real as the cry of a child?
A rabbit's cry may be wilder
But it has no soul.
Sugar can cure everything, so Kindness says.
Sugar is a necessary fluid,

Its crystals a little poultice.
O kindness, kindness
Sweetly picking up pieces!
My Japanese silks, desperate butterflies,
May be pinned any minute, anesthetized.

And here you come, with a cup of tea
Wreathed in steam.
The blood jet is poetry,
There is no stopping it.
You hand me two children, two roses.

WORDS

Axes
After whose stroke the wood rings,
And the echoes!
Echoes traveling
Off from the center like horses.

The sap
Wells like tears, like the
Water striving
To re-establish its mirror
Over the rock

That drops and turns,
A white skull,
Eaten by weedy greens.
Years later I
Encounter them on the road—

Words dry and riderless,
The indefatigable hoof-taps.
While
From the bottom of the pool, fixed stars
Govern a life.

CONTUSION

Color floods to the spot, dull purple.
The rest of the body is all washed out,
The color of pearl.

In a pit of rock
The sea sucks obsessively,
One hollow the whole sea's pivot.

The size of a fly,
The doom mark
Crawls down the wall.

The heart shuts,
The sea slides back,
The mirrors are sheeted.

BALLOONS

Since Christmas they have lived with us,
Guileless and clear,
Oval soul-animals,
Taking up half the space,
Moving and rubbing on the silk

Invisible air drifts,
Giving a shriek and pop
When attacked, then scooting to rest, barely
     trembling.
Yellow cathead, blue fish—
Such queer moons we live with

Instead of dead furniture!
Straw mats, white walls
And these traveling
Globes of thin air, red, green,
Delighting

The heart like wishes or free
Peacocks blessing
Old ground with a feather
Beaten in starry metals.
Your small

Brother is making
His balloon squeak like a cat.
Seeming to see
A funny pink world he might eat on the other side of it,
He bites,

Then sits
Back, fat jug
Contemplating a world clear as water.
A red
Shred in his little fist.

EDGE

The woman is perfected.
Her dead

Body wears the smile of accomplishment,
The illusion of a Greek necessity

Flows in the scrolls of her toga,
Her bare

Feet seem to be saying:
We have come so far, it is over.

Each dead child coiled, a white serpent,
One at each little

Pitcher of milk, now empty.
She has folded

Them back into her body as petals
Of a rose close when the garden

Stiffens and odors bleed
From the sweet, deep throats of the night flower.

The moon has nothing to be sad about,
Staring from her hood of bone.

She is used to this sort of thing.
Her blacks crackle and drag.

NOTES ON
POEMS
1956–1963

SPIDER. Anansi is the famous spider trickster hero of West African and Caribbean folklore. Towards the end of this year SP became interested in African folklore in general, with results that can be detected throughout the rest of her work.

1957

HARDCASTLE CRAGS. Valley of the Hebden River, a deep wooded gorge lying below the high road in the West Yorkshire moorland.

THE DISQUIETING MUSES. Reading this poem on a BBC radio programme, SP commented: 'It borrows its title from the painting by Giorgio de Chirico – *The Disquieting Muses.* All through the poem I have in mind the enigmatic figures in this painting – three terrible faceless dressmaker's dummies in classical gowns, seated and standing in a weird, clear light that casts the long strong shadows characteristic of de Chirico's early work. The dummies suggest a twentieth-century version of other sinister trios of women – the Three Fates, the witches in *Macbeth,* de Quincey's sisters of madness.'

OUIJA. SP occasionally amused herself, with one or two others, by holding her finger on an upturned glass, in a ring of letters laid out on a smooth table, and questioning the 'spirits'.

1959

THE BULL OF BENDYLAW. Cf. *English and Scottish Popular Ballads,* edited by F. J. Child (1883), where the following occurs as a 'fragment':

> The great bull of Bendy-law
> Has broken his band and run awa
> And the King and a his court
> Canna turn that bull about

ELECTRA ON AZALEA PATH. Azalea Path was the name of the cemetery path beside which SP's father's grave lies. On 9 March she wrote: 'A clear blue day in Winthrop. Went to my father's grave, a very depressing sight. Three graveyards separated by streets, all made within the last fifty years or so, ugly crude black stones, headstones together, as if the dead were sleeping head to head in a poorhouse. In the third yard, on a flat grassy area looking across a sallow barren stretch to rows of wooden tenements I found the flat stone: *Otto E. Plath: 1885–1940*. Right beside the path, where it would be walked over. Felt cheated. My temptation to dig him up. To prove he existed and really was dead. How far gone would he be? No trees, no peace, his headstone jammed up against the body on the other side. Left shortly. It is good to have the place in mind.'

On 20 March she wrote: 'Finished ... "Electra on Azalea Path". They are never perfect but I think have goodnesses.' And on 23 April: 'Must do justice to my father's grave. Have rejected the Electra poem from my book. Too forced and rhetorical.'

THE BEEKEEPER'S DAUGHTER. The detail in the last verse is mentioned in her father's book *Bumblebees and Their Ways*, and had been demonstrated to her by him.

POEM FOR A BIRTHDAY. In Boston, earlier in the year, she had tried for a way out through Robert Lowell's earlier manner of writing (as in 'Point Shirley'). She had always responded strongly to Theodore Roethke's poems, but it was only at Yaddo, in October, that she realized how he could help her. This sequence began as a deliberate Roethke pastiche, a series of exercises which would be light and throwaway to begin with, but might lead to something else. On 22 October she wrote: 'Ambitious seeds of a long poem made up of separate sections. Poem on her Birthday. [Her own birthday fell on 27 October.] To be a dwelling on madhouse, nature: meanings of tools, greenhouses, florists' shops, tunnels vivid and disjointed. An adventure. Never over. Developing. Rebirth. Despair. Old women. Block it out.' And then on 4 November: 'Miraculously I wrote seven poems in my "Poem for a Birthday" sequence. . . .'

MUSHROOMS. On 14 November: 'Wrote an exercise on Mushrooms yesterday which Ted likes. And I do too. My absolute lack of judgment when I've written something: whether it's trash or genius.'

1961

IN PLASTER. In March of this year SP spent a week in hospital undergoing an appendectomy. The patient in complete plaster lay on a neighboring bed. This and the next poem, 'Tulips', were written during this week.

THE MOON AND THE YEW TREE. The yew tree stands in a churchyard to the west of the house in Devon, and visible from SP's bedroom window. On this occasion, the full moon, just before dawn, was setting behind this yew tree and her husband assigned her to write a verse 'exercise' about it.

Speaking about this poem in a BBC radio broadcast, she said: 'I do not like to think of all the things, familiar, useful and worthy things, I have never put into a poem. I did, once,

243

put a yew tree in. And that yew tree began, with astounding egotism, to manage and order the whole affair. It was not a yew tree by a church on a road past a house in a town where a certain woman lived ... and so on, as it might have been in a novel. Oh no. It stood squarely in the middle of my poem, manipulating its dark shades, the voices in the churchyard, the clouds, the birds, the tender melancholy with which I contemplated it – everything! I couldn't subdue it. And, in the end, my poem was a poem about a yew tree. The yew tree was just too proud to be a passing black mark in a novel.'

1962

THREE WOMEN. This piece was written for radio at the invitation of Douglas Cleverdon, who produced it with great effect on the BBC's Third Programme, on 19 August 1962. The text was published by Turret Books in 1968, in a limited edition of 180 copies.

LITTLE FUGUE. Although never until now showing more than a general interest in music, about this time SP became keenly interested in Beethoven's late quartets, the Grosse Fuge in particular.

ELM. The house in Devon was overshadowed by a giant wych-elm, flanked by two others in a single mass, growing on the shoulder of a moated prehistoric mound.

This poem grew (21 sheets of working drafts) from a slightly earlier fragment:

> She is not easy, she is not peaceful;
> She pulses like a heart on my hill.
> The moon snags in her intricate nervous system.
> I am excited, seeing it there.

It is like something she has caught for me.

The night is a blue pool; she is very still.
At the center she is still, very still with wisdom.
The moon is let go, like a dead thing.
Now she herself is darkening
Into a dark world I cannot see at all.

These lines were a premature crystallization out of four densely crowded pages of manuscript. In her next attempt, some days later, she took them up and developed out of them the final poem 'Elm'.

THE BEE MEETING. SP kept one hive of bees, and attended meetings of the local Beekeepers Association. This poem draws on her experience of the first meeting she attended.

STINGS. The first stirring of this sequence of poems appeared on 2 August, when SP attempted to write a poem, which she never finalized in any way, titled 'Stings'. The following can be extracted from a mass of corrected manuscript:

What honey summons these animalcules?
What fear? It has set them zinging
On envious strings, and you are the center.
They are assailing your brain like numerals,
They contort your hair

Beneath the flat handkerchief you wear instead of a hat.
They are making a cat's cradle, they are suicidal.
Their death-pegs stud your gloves, it is no use running.
The black veil molds to your lips:
They are fools.

After, they stagger and weave, under no banner.
After, they crawl
Dispatched, into trenches of grass.
Ossifying like junked statues –
Gelded and wingless. Not heroes. Not heroes.

THE SWARM. When bees swarm, they sometimes cluster
in a ball high in a tree, while they make up their minds where
to go. Any loud sudden noise, such as gunfire, can make them
come down to a much lower level where the beekeeper can
reach them, and collect them into a box or skip. He then
shakes the whole lot out on to a broad surface that slopes up
into a fresh empty hive. The bees obediently march up into
the hive, as described towards the end of this poem.

The poet uses an incident she watched in a neighboring
beekeeper's garden.

THE APPLICANT. Introducing this poem in a reading pre-
pared for BBC radio, SP commented: 'In this poem, ... the
speaker is an executive, a sort of exacting super-salesman. He
wants to be sure the applicant for his marvelous product
really needs it and will treat it right.'

DADDY. In a reading prepared for BBC radio, she said of
this poem: 'Here is a poem spoken by a girl with an Electra
complex. Her father died while she thought he was God. Her
case is complicated by the fact that her father was also a Nazi
and her mother very possibly part Jewish. In the daughter
the two strains marry and paralyse each other – she has to
act out the awful little allegory once over before she is free
of it.'

FEVER 103°. In a BBC radio reading she prepared, SP intro-
duced this poem as follows: '[It] is about two kinds of fire –

the fires of hell, which merely agonize, and the fires of heaven, which purify. During the poem, the first sort of fire suffers itself into the second.'

She had made a somewhat earlier (but undated) attempt to break through to the substance of this poem. After several pages of what looks like feverish exploration of the theme, her earlier controls took over, and reduced the confusion to the following, which she left in manuscript, unfinalized:

> Four o'clock, and the fever soaks from me like honey.
> O ignorant heart!
> All night I have heard
>
> The meaningless cry of babies. Such a sea
> Broods in the newsprint!
> Fish-grease, fish-bones, refuse of atrocities.
>
> Bleached and finished, I surface
> Among the blanched, boiled instruments, the virginal
>   curtains.
> Here is a white sky. Here is the beauty
>
> Of cool mouths and hands open and natural as roses.
> My glass of water refracts the morning.
> My baby is sleeping.

BY CANDLELIGHT. The candlestick was a small brass image of Hercules, in his lion's pelt, kneeling under the candle. Behind his heels, five brass balls completed the design. (Cf. the poem 'Nick and the Candlestick'.)

ARIEL. The name of a horse which she rode, at a riding school on Dartmoor, in Devonshire.

NICK AND THE CANDLESTICK. 'In this poem,' she said

in a reading prepared for BBC radio, '. . . a mother nurses her baby son by candlelight and finds in him a beauty which, while it may not ward off the world's ill, does redeem her share of it.'

LADY LAZARUS. In a reading prepared for BBC radio, SP introduced this poem: 'The speaker is a woman who has the great and terrible gift of being reborn. The only trouble is, she has to die first. She is the Phoenix, the libertarian spirit, what you will. She is also just a good, plain, very resourceful woman.'

DEATH & CO. Introducing this poem in a reading prepared for BBC radio, she said: 'This poem is about the double or schizophrenic nature of death – the marmoreal coldness of Blake's death mask, say, hand in glove with the fearful softness of worms, water and other katabolists. I imagine these two aspects of death as two men, two business friends, who have come to call.'

The actual occasion was a visit by two well-meaning men who invited TH to live abroad at a tempting salary, and whom she therefore resented.

1963

SHEEP IN FOG. Introducing this poem in a reading prepared for BBC radio, SP said: 'In this poem, the speaker's horse is proceeding at a slow, cold walk down a hill of macadam to the stable at the bottom. It is December. It is foggy. In the fog there are sheep.'

It was first written on 2 December 1962. The last three lines of the original version were replaced by the present final three-line verse on 28 January 1963.

TOTEM. She explained this poem in conversation as 'a pile of interconnected images, like a totem pole'.

l. 5   *Dawn gilds the farmers...*: She imagines the West Country farmers in the early morning train, on their way up to London to the great meat market at Smithfield, whose 'white towers' she had been able to see from Primrose Hill during her first residence in London.

l.11   *In the bowl*...: A pyrex bowl, used on different occasions both for her son's afterbirth and the cleaned body of a hare.

l. 18   *a counterfeit snake*: an articulated toy snake of scorch-patterned bamboo joints.

THE 'ARIEL' POEMS
Sylvia Plath's own prepared collection of poems, titled *Ariel*, was ordered as follows:

INDEX OF FIRST LINES